What others say about this book:

What is there that is new that can be said about breastfeeding? Denise Punger surprised me and there is a lot that is new for me. It is so personal of a document. I am fascinated by some of the things she says. I particularly liked some of the reasons for bed sharing… The "safe" way, the way we approach breastfeeding, is not really the safe way. (It) robs many women of the extraordinary experience that breastfeeding can be, and the pleasure it usually gives to both the baby and the mother … Denise's book shows what can be done if we give breastfeeding a chance; the issue is finding the right approach for the baby (and mother) instead of the one size fits all approach that is too often the usual way.

– Jack Newman, MD, author of
The Ultimate Breastfeeding Book of Answers

(Dr. Punger) cracks me up. I appreciate how free she and her family are with issues that seem taboo in our society…really gives you that warm/attachment feeling.

– A Reader of Lactations.com

You've been such an inspiration to us all in SO many ways! It's almost like you've given us "permission" … to nurse just the way we want to, for how long we want to.

– Joan Fisher

Your work is such a contribution to all of us!

– Regina Sarah Ryan, author of
Breastfeeding: Your Priceless Gift to Yourself and Your Baby

My daughter will be healthier because of Dr. Punger.

– Shannon Miller

Information mothers need to consider prior to delivery. Insight to aid the medical professional to understand today's mothering movement.

– John Coquelet, DO

Your book makes me think about my next pregnancy, birth, and breastfeeding opportunity. I would listen more to my heart. I would think more about myself and not so much about what is convenient to others.

–Zaneta Defelici

It'll help me move on from my past birth. I've been thinking about doing something in regards to being a doula myself ... helping women birth the way they really want to.

–Catalina Bowen

PERMISSION TO MOTHER

Going Beyond the Standard-of-Care

to

Nurture Our Children

Denise Punger MD FAAFP IBCLC

Outskirts Press, Inc.
Denver, Colorado

Eternal G-d, open my lips, that my mouth may declare Your glory.

Permission to Mother
Going Beyond the Standard-of-Care to Nurture our Children

http://www.twofloridadocs.com
denisepunger@hotmail.com

Cover design by Melissa Jo Feuer
Cover Photo "Joan and Onika—In Tune with Nature" by Denise Punger
Back Cover "Proud of my Baby Brother" by Denise Punger
Back Cover "Carry Me like That" by Lisa Bell
Interior Photos by Denise Punger (and Family and Friends as credited)
Editor: Christie McKaskle

Outskirts Press, Inc.
http://www.outskirtspress.com

ISBN: 978-1-4327-0385-1

Library of Congress Control Number: 2007937506

Outskirts Press and the "OP" logo are trademarks belonging to Outskirts Press, Inc.

PRINTED IN THE UNITED STATES OF AMERICA

Dedication

To Adele Deutsch: A Mother to Us All
May, 10, 1925—December 19, 2004

Table of Contents

PAGE

PART 3 – BREASTFEEDING MEDICINE: MORE THAN PERMISSION

FOREWORD

The exquisite joy a mother feels at the first glimpse of her newborn is unmatched, a moment to be treasured forever. Unfortunately, that moment is increasingly robbed from a woman's maternal experience. Ever so slowly and insidiously, modern-day "knowledge" has poisoned the Truth: birth and breastfeeding are natural processes to be allowed to unfold as God ordained. This "modern" knowledge threatens to destroy our society's ability to parent our children as we begin to doubt our natural instincts to mother from birth.

At a time when the divide between natural childbirth and intervention-filled hospital birth is growing exponentially, women will covet the treasures shared in these pages. The last decade has seen phenomenal changes in the way Western society views birth and breastfeeding. Litigation and the need to control, both on the part of the parent and care provider, has played a large part in this change. Confidence in "the process" has eroded, as women have become victims of interventions meant to rescue them. Birth is now an event to be "medically managed," and feeding our children at the breast is viewed as an affront to modesty, an unnecessary sacrifice, or even child abuse when women breastfeed beyond toddlerhood.

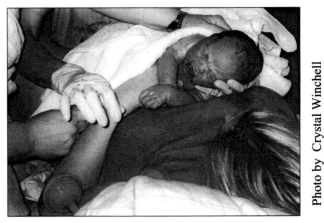

Photo by Crystal Winchell

The classic you are about to read will take you along Dr. Punger's personal journey from medical school training to home-centered parenting. Dr. Punger skillfully weaves her subjective experience as a mother with her clinical expertise as a family physician and international board certified lactation consultant. She examines birth and its outcomes in various elements, hospital and home, with and without professional doula support. Breastfeeding from the first moments of life to beyond the typical weaning years is chronicled together with the joys and difficulties women encounter personally and socially in feeding their young. Dr. Punger shares how her personal concern for her children's physical, mental, and emotional well-being leads her to a deeper involvement in their educational and spiritual foundation in the early years and beyond to a lifetime of learning.

At the time of our initial meeting, Dr. Punger was the expectant mom first and a physician second. I clearly remember her anxiety about her upcoming birth and my own concern as a doula serving this physician-mom. We put each other at ease during her second birth. The experience left me forever impressed that women are women when it comes to birth, and all of us can have positive birth experiences.

Dr. Punger has a way with putting life into words we can all relate to. She has amassed information covering a large, but very related set of mothering topics. If I could only put her words of wisdom in a nutshell and pour it into the hearts and minds of each of my "mothers," this world would be a better place.

For women of sensibility, this book will take you where you are in your journey of motherhood and give you a different way of looking at your unique circumstances. It will renew in you a sense of hope and wonder as you mother your children.

In the case of women who resist the path usually expected of today's mother, this book will make you an agent of change. As you allow the ripples of own life to affect those in your circle of influence, you will help to restore Godly confidence to women in their ability to mother their babies.

Bernadette Clark, RN, CD(DONA)
Wife to Jim, Mother to Twelve Blessings
Founder & President, Gentle Spirit Doulas
Founder & Editor, *Mother to Mother*

PREFACE

On my first day of medical school an anatomy professor told the whole freshman class that at least half of what we would learn in medical school would later be proven wrong. Later research, he said, often negates earlier research, which then changes the way we treat disease. My professor's disclaimer may have been the most useful tool I gained during all of my schooling. It continues to be useful to me, both as a doctor and as a mother. Inspired by what he taught, I have often been aware of what we think is best today, may be found to be less than best in the future.

Fortunately, my learning did not stop with medical school. Becoming a mother and joining a circle of mothers allowed me to experience what this professor meant. I heard birth stories that were full of regret. I also heard inspirational stories that conflicted with what I had been taught in med school about birth. Through time and my own experience I learned that having a baby is not "obstetrics." Having a baby is a real-life, deeply meaningful experience.

People who didn't know me before I had my three children often assumed that all my births were homebirths, and that it always was easy for me to trust my body to birth and nourish my children the way I do now. The truth is that only my third birth was a homebirth. I had given birth to my first two sons in hospitals.

The first birth was not satisfying. It was undermining and left me unfulfilled. I really went into that birth blind, especially relative to all the wisdom I have accumulated since. I was grateful that my obstetrician had patience with me that night, but for two years afterward I dwelled on what a demoralizing experience that birth was.

My second birth, two years later, was also a planned hospital birth. Still, that birth restored to me the trust that my body knows how to labor. It allowed me to regain confidence in myself. It helped that this time I had a doula that had had nine homebirths herself.

Most of my patients find it hard to believe that the field of obstetrics doesn't teach much about real-life pregnancy and birth and that pediatrics teaches next to nothing about breastfeeding beyond the first few days of life. Now, I share my own experience. I am grateful to have accurate memories, even of the "negative" events. I am grateful to be in a position to communicate them to you now.

For some time I have written and served as medical editor for a local doula publication called *Mother to Mother,* and I have included in this book updated and expanded material from my previous articles.

Part One tells my birth story, capturing my early perspective all the way through my sons' births and beyond. Part Two is about my breastfeeding years and includes much more than breastfeeding. Parts Three and Four are about extraordinary circumstances and some of the women that have done me an honor by allowing me to be a part of their new mommy experience.

A successful birth or successful breastfeeding relationship does not exist in a vacuum. Despite having my story divided into parts, understand that birth and breastfeeding influence each other. Breastfeeding success is a lifestyle, not a coincidence; thus, I write about how breastfeeding influences my life and how life influences my breastfeeding.

Professionally, I found that trying to solve early problems by dividing up the new family (with Mother going to the obstetrician and Baby to the pediatrician) *does not work*. Family Medicine was the best compromise until I found what I call Breastfeeding Medicine. There is no universal definition or single model for practicing Breastfeeding Medicine, but it's what keeps me professionally involved in both sides of birth.

This story is my journey. There is a chronological flow. The reader would benefit most from cover-to-cover reading. If you find it tempting, for example, to jump ahead to the anecdote on newborn jaundice, go ahead; but I recommend reading straight through to understand my thought process. I wonder if my professor knows how much his words influenced my life.

I write for mothers, because I have so much more to say than can be accomplished in a single office visit. Writing allows me to reach women that can't come in for an office consult due to distance or other extenuating circumstances. For women who choose to be active participants in their own healthcare during the childbearing years, I want you to enjoy and experience *Permission to Mother.*

PART 1 – CHILDBIRTH AS I EXPERIENCED IT

"Mom is your stomach going to stick out to Mars,"
-William and Scott

"What's a midwife?"
"You know that, William. She's the one who comes to deliver the baby."
"She delivers the baby? Or the baby comes out on its own?"

"All your friends are going to see you naked, hahahahahahaha."
"Will the baby be naked, too?"
William inquired upon realizing that I
would be almost naked during his brother's birth

William wants to support me when I am in labor. He wants to take the
pictures, turn on the music, and get the ice for my forehead to cool my
temper!!

"Scott, how will you help me if you are the only one home when the baby
wants to be born?"
"OH NO! I am not going to rub your back. It takes too long for the baby
to be born."

Kids are fascinated with learning the details of their birth,
"How old was I when I was born?" David questions.

Labor & Delivery in Medical School

My mother envisioned for me a future in health care, with babies, and she was right. My medical career began when I was a junior in high school. I volunteered in the radiology department of a metropolitan pediatric children's hospital. This rewarding experience as a candy striper led me to pursue employment in the nursery of a small community hospital.

It was no coincidence that I found the nursery job through my babysitting connections. I loved working alongside the physicians and nurses taking care of brand new families. There was quite a lot of action for a future doctor to observe, and it gave me encouragement to stay in school.

Our rural nursery provided a variety of care. We had healthy newborns that stayed with their moms. We also had babies who stayed in the nursery for treatment of jaundice with phototherapy or other types of monitoring. In case of respiratory distress we had emergency equipment to stabilize and transport out by helicopter. This always created a lot of excitement.

Many times, though, it was peaceful. We swaddled the newborns in receiving blankets and put them to sleep in the bassinets. Admirers could look through the big viewing window at the rows of newborns. This nursery was the all-American icon. Doesn't every parent dream of viewing their healthy, beautiful newborn through the nursery window?

My routine jobs included filling out the birth certificates, taking the highly prized newborn hospital photo, and handing out formula samples. These activities were more intertwined than you might think. The newborn photos we took were partly sponsored by the formula companies. This was one way for them to know when your baby was born and to know when to send you samples and age-appropriate adverzines. We alternated weeks to be fair to the companies. One formula company's discharge bags and samples were passed out one week; the competing company's bags went out the next week.

The La Leche League phone number was posted on a dusty sticky note next to the phone in case anyone called for breastfeeding help. Even back `then, I wondered, "Why do the doctors and nurses refer out for breastfeeding support? Don't they know how to help with breastfeeding?"

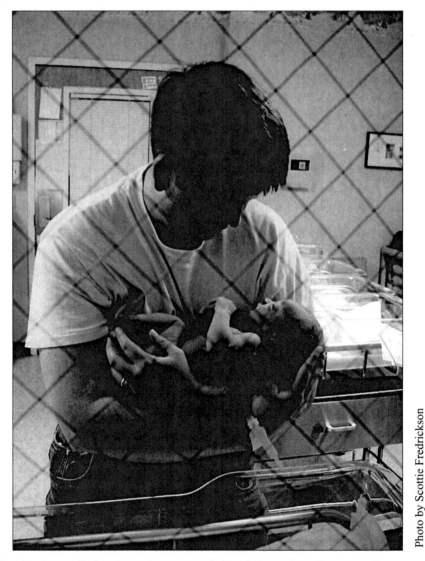

Photo by Scottie Fredrickson

Thinking back on all the times I answered the phones, I can't remember any calls for breastfeeding. Not too many mothers nursed, and I felt bashful around the few who did initiate breastfeeding in the hospital.

Working at this small community hospital as a high school senior gave me my first experience of labor and delivery. From the nursery, I could hear the laboring women suffer, and it made me cringe. Eventually, my empathy was suppressed because I was repeatedly told, "Once you see your baby, you forget it all."

After a baby was born, an L & D nurse brought the bundle to the nursery and put it under the warming lights. Every four hours we asked the mothers if they wanted to feed their own babies or if we should feed them in the nursery. I was young and never gave it a second thought. It was the hospital's routine, and I did not question authority.

I had my first experiences with birth during this employment. Twenty years later I found these cold, spiritless stories in my high school journal.

02/06/83

I have heard the crying and cursing of women in labor, but today was the first time I scrubbed to go into the delivery room. Mrs. F's baby was born at 11:59am and weighed 7-11. He was beautiful. Dr. R delivered him.

I was caught up with my responsibilities. I asked the head nurse if I could go in to see the next birth. She said that it was up to the doctor. I had heard from the nurses that Dr. R was one of the better OBs. He readily agreed to let me watch. I changed into scrubs.

Mrs. F was flat on her back on a table with her feet in stirrups and her legs spread apart. Fluid was dripping out of her vagina. I had to regroup and relocate her body parts because she was so edematous. Dr. R, all gowned up, poured Betadine on her and covered her legs with sterile gowns. He stuck his fingers all the way up her to find the baby's head. He cut a slit to make the birth canal bigger. He used forceps to pull him out. The mother did not have to push or concentrate on breathing. Blood gushed out everywhere. The baby was wiped off with towels. The umbilical cord was cut, and then mom could hold him. While she was admiring baby and crying, dad took pictures. Dr. R pulled the cord and placenta out and more blood gushed. The placenta was a sac with blood vessels and membranes. He used 4x4 gauze pads inside her to clean up so he could examine her. Her vagina seemed so big and stretched out; I could see right up inside. I was disoriented to what was what. He stitched her up. And the layers all came together. The baby had forceps marks on his face. I was told it would go away.

08/31/83

I had the privilege of attending a cesarean with Dr. H. This was the first time for me to go in the operating room. This room was very sterile. Bright lights from the ceiling and lots of scissors on the surgical tray caught my eye. They shaved and then sterilized Mrs. G's stomach with a rough brush and brown Betadine. Very methodically they covered her in sterile gowns. The nurse and surgeon were choreographed. They knew exactly where to make the folds in each drape and how to layer the towels. Dr. H cut a slit in her lower abdomen. He pulled the skin back with retractors. He cut the uterus and pulled the baby out. Lots of blood loss followed. A cautery was used to stop the bleeding. The smell of burnt tissue made me sick. They also stuffed towels in her so the pressure would encourage clotting.

The surgeon told me he had three layers to sew back up. He also told me that she had a catheter in her bladder to keep the bladder empty and flat because it is easy to "hit it." He told me the baby was breech. This was an emergency cesarean at 36 weeks. A happy ending the hospital staff said—a full term healthy baby. It didn't feel like a happy event.

I felt traumatized watching these births, so much so that I made this record of them. When I shared these stories with a friend and her husband, he showed me the forceps marks just above his temples. The scars never went away, and he was 32 years old when he showed them to me.

~♥~

When I imagined my future, I saw myself working with mothers and newborns. I couldn't decide whether I wanted to be the obstetrician and take care of mothers or the neonatologist that cares for newborns. I was disappointed to learn that there wasn't a medical specialty for people like me who wanted to care for both mother and baby.

To become a physician, a person generally takes four years of pre-med courses in college. Four years of medical school comes next, with the first two years covering the basic sciences. Finally, in the junior and senior years of medical school, the student does rotations in hospitals and clinics with real patients. After getting an MD degree, there is still an internship and residency to complete.

While in college, I commuted to work at the other hospital in our county system. I worked as a secretary on the medical/surgical floors and in the intensive care unit: wherever they needed me. Employment was necessary to pay for my education, but these jobs meant more to me than that. They provided me with the incentive to meet my career goals.

During those six years of employment I was exposed to many hospital services and had continual contact with the medical community. I was fortunate: Most of my peers did not have that hands-on patient contact during the premed and basic science years of our formal schooling. Throughout my medical education I clung to the memory of all the joy and satisfaction I found working with mothers and babies, as well as the hope that one day I would have something important to contribute to their well-being. During difficult semesters, this vision refueled my energy.

At long last I did my six-week core obstetric rotation at a community hospital. I worked with a surgical intern who was filling a requirement in obstetrics. He was very kind, and it was clear that he loved teaching, but he was still a surgeon; which means he liked surgery because he could "fix" things.

Some of the surgeons I worked under believed that the only real cure comes from G-d or surgery. They belittled the medical doctors who they perceived can only "care" and "control" illness, but not cure. I am not making this up; this is actually what I observed and was taught on my surgery rotation.

One of the OB attending physicians had subspecialty training in perinatology, so he spent a lot of time with ultrasound and amniocentesis to diagnose pathology in the unborn. Amniocentesis is the process where they stick a needle in a pregnant belly to get amniotic fluid. An ultrasound is used to guide the needle to pockets of fluid. I watched a lot of women subject themselves to this procedure without question. The attending claimed that the needle stick hurts less than a blood draw, but during my six-week rotation, there was one woman who lost her fetus after a routine amniocentesis.

While my attendings busied themselves with the monitor and data gathering, I enjoyed talking to the women who were going through all this. I liked the births and the rapport with new moms. All my associates noticed the relationships I formed and found me an important part of the team. My relational skills freed the surgeons to focus on their skills. I liked what I was doing. I didn't desire the ability to perform gynecological surgery—or any surgery, for that matter.

As a student, I didn't think to question how we did things. I watched hundreds of women get separated from their babies and families—saw them share labor and postpartum rooms with strangers—so that we could carry out our work. But the rotations met my expectations: They were designed to teach protocols and procedures. I observed that the residents, especially in surgical programs, love to do procedures. It is almost a contest, for example, to see whose laboring patient will "go first," who can rupture membranes (The protective layer around the baby soon to be born.) at only 2cm dilation, and who can get the required number of cesarean sections and instrumental deliveries in order to get hospital privileges.

My vision would always go back to the nursery, and the time finally came to do my nursery rotation. In the Neonatal Intensive Care Unit (NICU) I got to see what happened when babies were flown in from the community hospitals. Many of the babies we received were premature. Some were born with congenital problems that needed immediate attention. I continued to be inspired, but I didn't like being confined by technology. The NICU was too sterile and full of beeping machines. I felt cramped and claustrophobic, but at least I could walk out and take a break.

I felt sorry for babies in isolets who couldn't escape the noise. Some of them were in there for months. A photo of the family and a stuffed toy was supposed to make them "comfy." As much as I loved the babies, I didn't fit in the NICU.

The single greatest reason I had for not pursuing neonatology was simple. The noise gave me headaches. I have since wondered if I got headaches so quickly, what does all that noise do to the babies? I wonder if the light and noise pollution of that early environment causes some of the long-term behavioral problems we see in preemies?

The nursery wasn't the only place with noise pollution. L & D was, too. When the birthing woman is hooked up to electronic monitoring, and the volume, is turned up as it usually was, the baby's heart rate sounds like the three beat cadence of a horse's gallop. When several monitors were going at once, it reminded me of the Kentucky derby. My own adrenaline got going. I felt anxious and hurried. "Who would cross the finish line (give birth) first? Did our patients feel like they were horses pressured to perform? Once again, I found myself preferring a more peaceful atmosphere.

Eventually, I got to do a rotation in the intermediate nursery, which was a quieter environment. There was still too much focus on numbers; calorie counts, glucose levels, monitoring intake and output. I had a hunch about the potential and actual complications in newborns we were watching for. The complications actually seemed to be a result of our iatrogenic interference.

I did not realize this at the time, but I clearly understand now that not allowing a newborn to suckle at the breast leads to immediate problems like jaundice, low blood sugars, and feeding difficulties. Also contributing to "routine" problems of the newborn were the interventions performed on the pregnant and laboring mother.

I knew that experience in the nursery rotation was important in reaching my goals, but staying put wasn't what I was looking for. Instinctively, I knew that this wasn't where I could make the most positive impact on the lives of families.

Memories of my patients from being on-call with the obstetric department from those days have merged together into a generalized blur reminding me of the births I witnessed seven years earlier at work. Women came up to L& D in wheelchairs from the emergency room. They often stayed in the chair in the hallway until attended to. The labor rooms were semiprivate with curtain dividers: That means two patients shared a room, as well as a bathroom.

On admission everyone got an enema and a shave. Everyone's fetal heart tones and contractions were monitored, first externally with belts to hold the monitors in place. Many got internal electrodes. Internal electrodes to monitor the unborn's heartbeat meant that a tool that coiled like a wire cork screw was inserted beyond the mother's vagina and past the dilating cervix into the womb. It was literally twisted into the baby's scalp, many times leaving bruises and scabs. The woman's water had to be broken to put in this scalp electrode. This was all done in between contractions, and it was thought that this was a more accurate way to monitor the baby.

Televisions were usually on. There was no peace or privacy for laboring. All the patients "needed" pitocin and epidurals. We were taught the typical length of labor for a first-timer as opposed to a mom who'd already given birth before and there was no accounting for individual differences. Everyone was supposed to fit the bell curve. No one was given the space to let her labor happen in its own time.

We did vaginal exams every two hours to check for cervical dilation. An attending and I would both do the exam each time. There was a cervical dilation chart on the wall so we students could remember how many finger breaths each dilation was. What an inappropriate focal point for our laboring patients, conveniently located opposite the head of the bed!

I recall a few 13-year-olds in labor. They automatically got epidurals, because they "couldn't handle it." I also remember a few physicians who got epidurals for comfort and dignity usually before active labor had a chance to begin. (No wonder physicians have high rates of C-sections.) Everyone else got epidurals, too, even if there wasn't a special circumstance.

Women both labored and began pushing in these semiprivate rooms. To "help" with the pushing, two staff members would be on either side of the bed, pressing the women's knees into her chest while she lay on her back, holding her breath, while we counted to ten and stared at her bottom. We'd tell her to "Breathe," another count from us, and then she could relax.

When she was crowning we moved the laboring woman onto a stretcher, took her down the hall without privacy (telling her not to push despite the urge), and scooted her onto a new table prepared with sterile drapes. It was here she was to give birth. We transferred women twice during this imminent stage of birth. It was as if we thought of birth as two distinct processes; labor and delivery.

This type of thinking rationalized the transfer to another bed and to another room. While the nurses were transferring the lady, we physicians went to the sink for our "ritual." We scrubbed with Betadine brushes up to our elbows and underneath every fingernail. We covered our shoes, hair, and faces in sterile gowns and latex gauntlets.

When we met the birthing mother back in the delivery room, her feet were already in stirrups on the sterile gurney. Betadine was used to clean the perineum, callously poured by the nurse. No stool came out with pushing, because Mom had had an enema long ago in labor. She'd also probably been catheterized several times to empty her bladder. Drapes were set up over her legs and below her to protect the sterile field and to catch the blood and amniotic fluid.

The nurse busied herself by keeping up with the fetal heart tones on the mother's abdomen with the monitor as the baby descended downward. If a woman had an epidural in place, it was convenient to do an episiotomy. (I sound casual about it, but that's how I remember it being explained.) If not, we had to give her a local anesthetic right into the perineum. Often we injected a local as she was pushing!

Despite all of that, it was still amazing to watch a baby's head emerge as the vaginal walls crown the baby's head and the head "makes it to the outside." With the baby halfway in and halfway out, we paused at the neck to make sure the cord wasn't wrapped around it. If so, we manually moved the cord out of the way. Some babies needed to be orally suctioned before the body delivered if there was thick meconium. Then we allowed the rest of the body to deliver with the next urge to push.

We examined the cervix and perineum right away. The thinking was, "While the mothers are admiring their babies, they won't notice what we do." While waiting for the placenta to deliver, we could check for tears on the perineum, labia, or cervix. Checking the cervix is quite invasive. We used two fingers from one hand to stretch the vaginal walls and make room for a retractor and/or sponge clamp in order to visualize the cervix.

Most of my patients did not get cut. I also had the understanding that tears healed up better than episiotomies did. I was relieved to see a baby born over an intact perineum. I really did not enjoy suturing a new mom.

The cord was clamped off and cut with surgical scissors without haste. The placenta's delivery was managed by "fundal massage." That means massaging the top of the uterus palpable through the abdominal wall. The partner could be at mom's side, but not in the sterile field. "We" always caught the baby and cut the cord.

Often there was a pediatric resuscitation team present. The team could provide emergency oxygen, suction, intubation and cardiac compressions. Once they were pronounced healthy, babies could be given to their mothers. But that didn't last long. To get the party moving out of the delivery room, we took the baby back. "We've got to weigh him now," we said. And that got the babies into the nursery before their mothers could "spoil" them. We also had a nurse ready to give eye ointment and vitamin K at the first opportunity.

The placenta was sent to pathology for further examination once we had examined it.

I viscerally recoiled from this "management." Still, I knew no other way. This was, more or less, how I was taught by the obstetricians to "deliver" babies. "Even if these women don't seem to mind, I am never going to have a baby," I thought. There were, of course, minor variations in procedure from birth to birth. But for the most part this is the procedure we generally followed when "all was well." This is what we called normal spontaneous vaginal birth. When birth was complete we moved Mom to a recovery area before going out to the floor in yet another room.

I have a few scattered memories of specific births I witnessed in those days, none of which involved breastfeeding.

Once I made the "mistake" of being there to catch a baby barehanded on the transport table in the hall. The mom had five babies before and could not hold back. It was not a sterile birth. Looking back at it, it was the first natural birth I witnessed. Mom and baby both did well.

One heartbreaking night, another woman came in with fetal loss at 36 weeks. The OB resident "delivered" the baby, and I provided emotional care to the mother. No one wanted my job, but I knew I played critical a role.

I remember another lady who delivered twins. Twin A was delivered vaginally, but Twin B was delivered by emergency cesarean, probably because of transverse or breech presentation. That mom went through a lot, and I wasn't comfortable with how casually the cesarean was treated.

The scheduled cesareans, on the other hand, went by quickly. I saw mothers walk into the hospital dressed and made-up, feeling nothing. Then they'd don their hospital gowns, lie on a gurney, have major surgery and finish with a baby in their arms. This didn't seem like the miracle of birth to me. Not that the other births did, but I sensed even more loss in the "scheduled" transition from pregnancy to motherhood and a loss in early bonding time.

Another woman pushed her baby out and pushed her uterus out with it, inside out! The uterus literally had to be pushed back inside. We gave her facemask anesthesia to knock her out. These emergency situations stimulated the OB residents. But I didn't find it exciting. The moral of this story was, "Birth is dangerous." Actually, that was the moral of *every* birth in obstetric training.

Despite the fear of birth, it was not a big deal to deliver a "vaginal birth after cesarean," as long as the uterus had a horizontal incision. We checked prior birth records, but other than that there was no restriction and nothing we did different to manage labor.

Seven years after working in that first nursery, I finally did my Family Medicine rotation at the Army base. My work included newborns, obstetrics and much more. It was an eye opener. It made me realize that pediatricians are not the only ones who take care of babies, and obstetricians are not the only ones to take care of pregnant woman (although some may think they are the only ones qualified to). Furthermore, I learned that perinatologists are not the only ones who can handle medical problems during pregnancy. Family Medicine seemed to have the most potential to combine all of my interests, including prevention. Prevention—now there's an idea that grabbed my attention.

Beyond my core courses, I did most electives in OB and Neonatology, departments that kept me close to the reproductive needs of women. When it came time to make a decision about what specialty I would pursue, I chose Family Medicine. Family Medicine residents get exposure to the full range of medicine, including both obstetrics and pediatrics. We provided prenatal care for our patients who conceived, and we also had the privilege of taking care of their newborns. This continuity, I loved! For an obstetrician, birth is the end of a nine-month patient-physician relationship. To me, birth is the beginning of a family unit. By choosing to go into Family Medicine, I got to be a part of that new family.

FAMILY MEDICINE WITH OBSTETRICS

My medical school rotations had involved women facing high-risk births. They had a variety of issues. Some had a multitude of medical problems such as diabetes or hypertension that required medications during labor. Others had fetal problems like congenital heart defects that required a team of specialists to be available at birth. Complications due to HIV or addiction are all too common at teaching hospitals, and mine was no exception. Obstetrical rotations are designed to prepare a physician to handle the most difficult births.

As I began my residency in FP with OB I began to learn to question the routine "standard-of-care." The women who came to family physicians were low-risk compared to the high-risk ladies that had been referred to the obstetricians I trained with before. Family doctors didn't need to rely so much on surgical skills or routines. This introduced me to the idea that *the "routine" interventions are not necessary for all patients.*

My department recognized birth as a significant event in the life of a woman instead of a medical problem. Yet that recognition didn't go far enough. I walked away with the message that having a decorated birthing room, playing music and avoiding the shave and enema met most women's needs.

It is hard to change a mind-set you have carried up to this point in your life. Alternatives to hospital birth were certainly not addressed in my training. I thought birth centers and midwifery were for eccentric types, not professionals like me. The doula phenomenon was just barely emerging. I don't remember ever discussing homebirth except in a derogatory way. The assumption was that homebirths were precipitous and unplanned, or maybe for people we judged as too stupid to know they were pregnant. Unfortunately for the majority of expectant mothers, this close-minded approach is typical of physician training.

One of my pregnant patients during residency opened my eyes. She was exceptional. Jayne was a single lawyer who had a birth plan and advocated for her right to have a natural delivery. My first thought was "An attorney! I should refer her to an OB. They'll know a lot more about what to do for her than I do." I was curious and open to her views, but I didn't think her needs could be met in our hospital. Could I, a third-year Family Medicine resident, protect her birth plan?

I looked forward to Jayne's appointments because I always learned so much. She came with tons of questions raised by the parenting books she read. I couldn't answer the questions, which sure raised my curiosity. At this point, I had read many of the standard obstetric texts. What could a lay book add that I didn't already know? It wasn't until years later, when I read these books as a parent, that I saw their value. Now, I have a list of recommended reading for families.

This is one of the first lessons I learned from Jayne. During one early prenatal appointment, I scheduled an amniocentesis for her even though she was barely over 36. You don't have to have special training to know the common OB equation that "age > 35 = amniocentesis."

Fortunately, my faculty attending physician noticed that Jayne had a normal ultrasound and normal triple screen. Why was I scheduling the amnio, he asked. Had I discussed it with her? Had I let her know that amniocentesis had risks? Had I thought to ask her if she even wanted to know the results? The attending reminded me that not all women want to know. Even if a genetic defect is discovered, many want to love and cherish their babies no matter what. So I went back and talked to Jayne. After informed discussion she chose to pass on the amniocentesis. This was the difference in having a Family Practice instructor whose perspective was different from the perinatologist, I previously trained with.

At another appointment, Jayne announced that she would have a female companion to support her throughout labor. I thought this was a good idea since Jayne's partner wasn't involved in her pregnancy and she had no family in the area. I couldn't know the impact this choice would eventually have on me, or that I'd eventually come to believe all laboring woman should have a doula. As her due date came closer, I became anxious about Jayne's delivery. I wanted to be certain that I was there for her. Finally she called to say that she was having strong, regular contractions. At that point in residency, I encouraged my patients to stay at home as long as possible. "The longer you stay home, the less the hospital can do to you."

But soon it was time for Jayne to come in. Hoping to get there first, I approached the elevator and saw Jayne in a wheelchair panting through a contraction with a support person who knew exactly what to do for her. This was the first time I had ever seen anything like it. It was always awkward being with a laboring woman in so much need, but not knowing how to provide comfort. The only ways I knew to deal with pain were to cover it up or speed it up. I could catch babies, but, honestly, I don't think Jayne and her coach even needed me.

As I approached the elevator, I called out, "Hold the door! I'm her doctor." It's unfortunate that Jayne didn't deliver in the elevator. By the time she got to her room, nurses were ready to start an IV and strap the monitor around her, even though the baby's head was crowning. She was a first-time mother and couldn't push that baby out quick enough for the persistent staff to do their procedures. I told them to leave her alone, that pushing the baby out would end the pain. They passed me the Betadine and razor, which I didn't want to use. They argued with me, "What if she tears?"

I said, "I'll worry about it then." I did repair a tear and did not need to trim away any hair. Her coach provided comfort and reassurance throughout the process, something I couldn't do while stitching. It came naturally to me to acknowledge Jayne's effort and her beautiful newborn. After that, I made it a point to commend all my mothers on their labor. I also told them how beautiful their newborns were. I realized that this validation would help bonding and perhaps compensate for the hospital's inadequacies.

As I remember it, Jayne was the first patient I ever had who wanted to breastfeed for at least a year. She actually looked forward to breastfeeding. How intimidating to me! But I pretended I wasn't fazed. The only thing I had learned about breastfeeding came from a poster in the Tri-County Health Clinic. "Breastmilk," it said. "Healthier, neater, cheaper and smarter." I was thankful that Jayne had no problems, because I had no skills to deal with breastfeeding complications and wouldn't have known who to ask for help.

As FP residents, we were encouraged to keep strict logs of procedures, so that if we ever requested hospital OB privileges, we could demonstrate that we had enough experience. I logged Jayne in, even though I really didn't do much for her. But I never forgot her because I learned the most from her.

I held in high esteem those Family Medicine faculty and the other residents that kept obstetrics in their practice. I'm quite sure my attendings and colleagues would have voted me "Most Likely to Do FP with OB."

~♥~

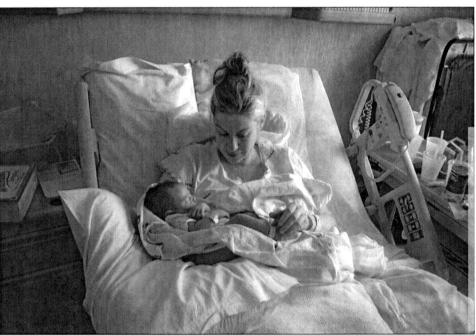

Photo submitted by Shannon Miller

What I learned from Jayne I passed along to Arlene. She was a pre-med classmate of mine, and I had introduced her to her husband, Pierre. She had graduated and was now one of my few peers to have a baby during my residency. The rest of us were too busy studying. Arlene's pregnancy was just a few months behind Jayne's.

Because Pierre was on faculty in the Anesthesiology Department, Arlene was privileged to get her prenatal care from one of the "highfalutins" in the OB department. As my friend, Arlene gave me updates on her prenatal appointments. Often, these updates allowed her to vent her dissatisfaction with the information she was getting. So I shared what I would do for Jayne at an equivalent point in pregnancy. I also had a few articles and pointers to give her to share how FPs did things.

Late in her pregnancy, it was clear to Arlene that she went to her appointments just for the measurements; then she came to me for "the rest of the story." Finally growing tired of not getting the care she needed, Arlene made a previously unheard-of decision. At about 35 weeks into her pregnancy, she transferred her care to me. Out of the OB's practice into the care of a family medicine resident!

It just goes to show you that it's never too late to get the provider you want. And rank has nothing to do with quality of care.

Jayne and Arlene were very special to stand out the way they did.

~♥~

Before I finished my residency there was talk about the new room for labor and delivery. The bed could be adjusted into an upright position to be like a birth stool. Transport down the hall could be eliminated. You had to meet special low risk qualifications to be allowed to deliver in this more home-like room. That's all I remember, except that some of my family medicine attendings insisted upon using this room.

Towards the end of residency, I did office work for an exemplary Family Practitioner who does obstetrics in an outlying rural town. I've always imagined that he practiced the way I might want to. I probably would have enjoyed "FP with OB" if I had stayed in the area.

There were different perspectives and lots of controversies about protocols as I was exposed to different hospitals. I remember disagreements with how our Family Practice department did things compared to the OBs. Although every ounce of my attention was given to pregnancy and birth during residency, I was more consciously questioning whether I could physically stand to do obstetrics.

As it turned out, my husband and I moved to South Florida after residency was completed. Rather than pursue a "high risk specialty" in a new state and new community, we both accepted urgent care jobs. It was refreshing to have set hours and not worry about being on call.

There are many parts of the country where family doctors include obstetrics in their practice and make an important contribution by doing so. However, among family doctors, the decision to give up obstetrics at the end of residency usually meant giving it up for life. Although I enjoyed a slower pace of living and working, I missed the involvement with women and their health issues. Something in me knew that I would find my way back. And I did: I became a mother and went through the experience myself.

Photo by William Coquelet, age 6

CHILDBIRTH – IT'S MY TURN

Having my own birth stories has helped me listen to other mother's stories in a different way. I really listen, more than just "take a medical history." My respect for pregnancy and birth, already enormous, has increased even more. I am thoroughly convinced that birth forever changes everything about a woman. I have seen for myself that an empowering experience improves a mother's emotional and physical health. On the other hand, undermining a woman's ability to birth will adversely affect her health. Her birth experience can have a profound impact not only on the way she raises her children, but also on how she relates to her partner, family and friends.

So I am constantly amazed (though no longer surprised) by how much the actual birth is overlooked by our culture. My expectant patients often put more thought into their nursery themes than their birth plans. I have heard a lot of theories to explain this. For some, it may be about valuing material goods over experiences. Some women just don't believe they can have a bad experience with birth. Some even think that using an epidural or scheduling a cesarean section negates the need for a birth plan. But women planning surgery or intervention need even more support, because they are at greater risk for complications. No one should ignore the information and help available.

Childbirth was not quite what I had expected. I knew it would be tough, but I thought that my optimism, insight, medical education, good health and family support would get me through labor with dignity. If not, it didn't matter, because I was still under the impression women are supposed to "forget it all afterward." Four years later, when I was asked to write about my first two births, I could remember both in vivid detail.

I wish our culture would encourage women to talk about how the birth experience makes us feel, not just the sequence of events. Both my pregnancies raised feelings in me that I had never heard other women or physicians talk about in any depth. My first birth was a typical hospital birth that left me unfulfilled. Fortunately, I was much better prepared the second time, when I hired a doula for physical and emotional support.

MY FIRST LABOR

My first labor began around 4 a.m. after a long nine months. The very first identifiable contraction to wake me up felt like diarrhea cramps. The next few contractions felt similar. Seeing that I was not sick, I recognized this to be labor. Instead of going back to sleep, which was the first mistake (I had no idea how long a day I was facing), I picked up one of my favorite novels and read. I was relaxed. In the beginning, I was hopeful and in control. I found comfort being in my house. I passed time in a warm Jacuzzi bath. I was reassuring John and my mother most of the day. After twelve hours of easy, rhythmic contractions, they were getting anxious. I thought I had to be making progress and could go in to "deliver." I wanted to confirm my suspicion by checking myself internally for my baby's descent. My cervix was still very high and hard to reach. This discouraged me. It had been a long day of no sleep and little food for all of us. John's mother, who was also with us, was anxious in her own way. When the contractions started getting stronger, they began to coax me into going to the hospital sooner than I had wanted.

The intake nurse, getting ready to check my cervix for progress said, "You know I *have* to do this" and prompted me to lie down on my back. She *knew* it was not in my best interest to interrupt my laboring instincts, but she was following hospital protocol. I hesitated to follow her command. As I went with the flow of a contraction all alone, she became pushy. I gave in.

I put on the hospital gown, followed instructions on the nurse's timetable, and answered admission questions. My dilation had progressed since coming in, but not as far as I would have thought. Following the hospital's agenda seemed to interrupt my labor forces so much that I couldn't recover.

The hospital room felt like it was 100 degrees. I couldn't get into a comfortable position. With the onset of unexpected vomiting and more stronger contractions, all optimism was gone. The perfectly centered clock on the wall, which became my unwelcome focal point, reminded me how slowly time was passing. I was fatigued, famished and in pain. I was also without experienced; let alone any emotional and physical support. It didn't matter anymore how many years I had attended medical school, nor that I'd had the experience of delivering babies. I became as helpless as any hospital patient in labor.

Some friends of John were in the waiting room, and I had not expected their presence. I knew they could hear me because I could hear the cursing howls of a woman laboring in another room. The lack of privacy further inhibited my efforts to focus.

My "pushing stage" lasted three hours. I use the term lightly: I was waiting for the urge to push and never did feel it. I hadn't known this stage could last over two hours. In residency, the patients I saw ended up with a vacuum or forceps-assisted delivery, or cesarean section, if this stage lasted very long. It felt like one long contraction that would never end. There was no time to recover from the previous contraction.

I remember everyone eagerly watching my bottom, hoping a head would emerge. I was worried that I might push out stool, and this also hindered my efforts to focus. I didn't know yet that stool would have been a good sign because it would have meant my pushing was effective. Being flat on my back with legs spread open didn't help me feel safe. After some time, my obstetrician saw how powerless and ineffective I felt lying down. He encouraged me to get up and lean over a birth bar to have gravity work with me. I liked being upright because my perineum wasn't the focus in this position, but it was too late.

John and my mother were worn out after 16 hours, when I needed them the most. I had believed that husbands and mothers made great labor support. In a traditional culture, this may be true, but today most men have never seen a woman in labor, and most of our mothers were sedated when we were born. Hospital prenatal classes teach us to pick a coach like your husband or mother and bring that person to class, so that both will know what to expect at the hospital. The classes don't empower you to be in control, nor do they emphasize the importance of having an experienced female with you who has gone through natural birth herself.

After so many hours of pushing, I begged my obstetrician to stop the pain any way he could. It was humiliating to cry for the end. I cried for anything: the vacuum, forceps, episiotomy, cesarean section. It didn't matter at that point. I thought I would be better off dead.

Looking back, I am grateful that my doctor respected my initial plan (another physician might have been quicker to change course) and waited for William to be born vaginally. At the end, the nurse put an oxygen mask on me, which seemed to energize me to push when instructed.

After the birth was over, my doctor agreed to let William nurse while he continued on with his work. While holding William for the first time, I was aware of everything my OB did. I could feel the needle being injected and the burning infiltration of Lidocaine into my perineal tissue. I had forgotten that after giving birth a woman often shivers from all the changes in body fluids. I was supposed to lie still for the obstetrician to check my cervix and repair my tear!

The majority of women would have had an epidural by now and may not be aware of what was going on. My OB probably wasn't used to someone who was miserable, but sensitive and sober at this point. I was politely reminded by my OB, "Denise, you know you have to be still for this."

Before I knew what was happening, I involuntarily responded by kicking him. Then came the IV pain medication; I was medically restrained and put out of my misery. My OB could finish the suturing.

Indifferent to my needs, or just thinking I was finally out of it and wouldn't remember, they pulled my soiled gown off. I laid stark naked, feeling very exposed for eternity, so it felt, before one of them took the initiative to drape me. Why doesn't anyone ever talk about how violating that time after the birth is? Labor was over, and the family's focus was on the newborn. Who was looking out for me then?

For the next several days it felt like my body had been physically beaten. My mother went back home, telling me that I would "feel better soon." My husband went back to work after two days. It seemed like everyone quickly forgot my labor. Feeling alone, I wondered if I was the only woman who was traumatized by her own labor. Was I the only one who felt this way? Was this how my patients felt?

My mother later shared with me that she thought my hollering and lack of control was abnormal behavior. At the time, the comments added insult to my injury. Now I realize that my mother had never seen another birth and had no point of reference. Besides, I was also concerned that my behavior was abnormal: I was embarrassed to face my obstetrician at my six-week check up.

I wish that there had been an experienced female labor coach to tell us that my labor was normal for me, and that I did a great job pushing out a nine-pounder. I wish that someone could have helped me get into different positions so that I was not lying on my back with my bottom exposed to the world for hours. If I'd had an experienced labor assistant, I might not have walked away from this birth experience frightened to have another pregnancy. Now I know that I did the best I could under the circumstances.

PREGNANT A YEAR LATER

I couldn't believe I was pregnant again. I wanted another baby, but I didn't want to endure three hours of pushing and losing my dignity again. When I shared my feelings with my midwife, she recommended calling a doula.

The right doula would certainly have a job cut out for her. I was so convinced that no one could really help me. I thought it would be too easy for a lay person to be intimidated by me and my husband. Also, I had strong convictions about nursing while pregnant. At my 32-week prenatal visit a female OB covering for my usual doctor warned me emphatically to stop breastfeeding. She thought it would lead to early labor.

My research easily disproved this kind of thinking, but I still needed to be surrounded by people who were supportive of me. So the next week, when I interviewed a doula named Bernadette, I intentionally encouraged William to nurse during the interview (as if he wouldn't nurse on his own). I had decided that if this doula said anything negative about my nursing or seemed uncomfortable with it, I'd move on.

It turned out that Bernadette was tandem nursing her youngest two boys. Wow, I didn't expect that. I needed her example for breastfeeding too. My husband and I felt better as soon as we met Bernadette, and she felt good about us. We signed her contract and sent a check right away.

After my traumatic labor and delivery with William, this birth would be a chance to prove to myself that my body was normal. Bernadette seemed to know how to help. She helped us to realize how common it is for men to get tired, nervous, and pale seeing their partner's labor. John felt relieved that he could play the role of a nervous father-to-be and not be 100 percent responsible for my pains, emotional state and birth memories. Nor would he have to starve and hold his bladder for the entire labor!

BIRTH WITH A DOULA

My second labor did not start until my 41st week, which gave me seven extra days to dwell on the upcoming event. Bernadette let me call her any time. She was always encouraging and put my mind at ease.

One night around midnight, my membranes ruptured. This didn't alter my plans. I was still going to stay home as long as I could. At first I thought it might be urine, but I folded a cloth baby diaper in my panties. With each contraction I continued to feel a little trickle of fluid. I knew this would be the night.

Because my family was asleep, I had some privacy and time without anyone (not family, not nurses, not OBs) nagging me, "Are you sure you're having contractions?" Perhaps my body felt safer to start labor with everyone asleep. Many expectant women might not let their partners sleep through any of labor; but for me, experience changed the priorities. This way, John would be awake, attentive and supportive to me in the early morning, when Scott was born. Besides, I also wanted to cuddle, nurse and cherish William. Soon he would have to share me with his baby brother.

Bernadette arrived an hour after I called her. Early in my labor, we walked around the block. The midnight air was refreshing. I felt camaraderie between the two of us. She told me that I made it look easy. Bernadette reminded me to sip liquids frequently and to empty my bladder. Sitting on the toilet served another purpose. We automatically relax our pelvic muscles when we sit. Relaxed muscles meant that the baby would move down quicker. Sitting in the bathroom really seemed to make labor progress.

Bernadette had a soothing voice, a quality that my family lacked. She taught me how to listen to my body to know what stage of labor I was in. I did not need or want discouraging vaginal exams. We laughed as I ceremoniously deposited a few stretched out maternity clothes into the garbage. I was social and optimistic, a sign of early labor.

At about 4 a.m. the contractions became much stronger. I found that the kitchen counter was good support to lean on. Bernadette knew exactly where to apply counter-pressure on my back, and the pain instantly diminished. It was amazing to be so aware of the sensations I was experiencing!

As my family gathered, I wanted to stay focused. I was irritable with their interruptions and blamed everyone for my pain, a common behavior in active labor. They didn't seem to understand how much I needed to and wanted to concentrate. Bernadette assured us that labor was progressing well, and that my irritability was normal. She reminded us of the incredible work my body was doing. Her gentle voice continued to calm all of us.

In addition to the physical and emotional support I hired her for; Bernadette brought something beyond my expectations—her trust in G-d's design for birth. This perspective on birth was quite novel compared to the obstetrical view! Even though I didn't yet understand her point of view, I knew she had given birth ten times before. All the wisdom and experience she shared with me was comforting.

In medical school, we determined dilation by an internal exam. As a physician, I was never taught to observe a woman's body language, mood and verbal clues to help evaluate her closeness to birth. But now, I knew I had reached transition and was close to birth because I felt renewed energy, a trembling in my legs and buttocks, and *the urge to push!*

We took off for the hospital. I had several hard contractions in the car. I was on all fours in the back seat going with each contraction. John and Bernadette were up front riding. In route, I had their verbal support, but not their physical contact. I experienced my second to last contraction while entering the hospital. Instinctively (I had never seen this done before), I grabbed Bernadette and let her support me as I went into a semi-squat. It felt so good to be out of the car and to surrender with support. This was painful but powerful. I felt my baby's head crowning during this contraction. I could touch his head with my hand. My hands were the first to touch him. There was enough time in between contractions to make it to the delivery room. At the start of the next contraction, I warned them, "Scott is coming, now!" I should have kept quiet.

I started to semi-squat with Bernadette, but a nursed motioned me to lie on the bed. "You are not going to deliver this baby on the floor," she ordered. They managed to get me in the bed while I was contracting, not exactly letting me follow my instincts, like the contraction before. But, indeed, Scott delivered his entire body on the first contraction in the delivery room. A midwife from another group happened to be there and caught him. Another nine-pound baby. As I held him, tears filled my eyes. Relief, joy, happiness, empowerment, love, renewal. I am not sure which emotion prevailed over me the most.

I had uncomfortable afterbirth contractions. I shivered while a tear was being repaired and a cervical exam was conducted. Bernadette stayed with us until I was stable and comfortable. William had been a natural at nursing, but since I'd be nursing two now, she wanted to stay a little longer and make sure my breastfeeding relationship with Scott got off to a good start. Bernadette also came to check on us several days later.

What else do I remember about giving birth with the help of a doula? Being in control the entire time. Giving birth without medical intervention and hearing positive affirmations throughout my labor. I had no vaginal exams during this labor, no electronic fetal monitoring, no race to the finish line. I was free to ambulate and encouraged to eat, drink, and eliminate the entire time! I even birthed in my own clothes. All that said, it was the ability to welcome and surrender to the contractions on my own terms that allowed me to spontaneously heal from my first birth experience. I could not have done that without my doula.

~❤~

I am often asked why I didn't want an epidural. Practically speaking, I feared epidurals more than I feared labor. I feared it would enter the wrong space, and I'd have a stroke. I couldn't imagine volunteering to take a huge needle into my back. I've done enough spinal taps to know how easy it is to miss.

Scientifically speaking, my review of the research has indicated that epidurals lengthen labor and increase the chance of other interventions, which in turn lead to an increased chance of c-sections. Moreover, the long-term effects of epidurals are not well known. I didn't want to take a chance on anything interfering with breastfeeding and bonding.

Spiritually speaking, an epidural denies you the chance to experience giving birth as the journey it truly is. In a way, I wish the obstetrician from my first birth had been at Scott's birth. He would have seen the difference a doula could make. If I delivered babies, I would insist that all my patients must hire a doula. It makes me sad to hear one mother tell another, "You'll forget it all, anyway." Giving birth can be a rewarding physical, emotional, and spiritual experience, one you will never forget.

FINDING BREASTFEEDING MEDICINE

From the time Scott was born I had become increasingly involved in the breastfeeding community. Breastfeeding came fairly easily for me. It broke my heart to see how many mothers received wrong information and weaned unnecessarily when they had problems. I began attending local La Leche League (LLL) meetings, the mother's breastfeeding support group. I also presided over the Breastfeeding Task Force, the local breastfeeding advocacy group.

I discovered that LLL Medical Associates held annual conferences that also tolerated the presence of quiet nursing babies. Since I needed to meet continuing education requirement, these were perfect for me. The first breastfeeding conference I went to exclusively for physicians was an eye-opener. My medical training encouraged me to "support" breastfeeding, but it had not prepared me to help breastfeeding pairs when problems arouse. I learned there was so much more I could do to help mothers than I had ever envisioned.

I attended the LLL Medical Associates Annual Conference two years in a row. I became aware of the need for a specialty devoted exclusively to the unique needs of breastfeeding mothers and their babies. When I discovered that a few (less than 10, if that many) physicians in North America were practicing breastfeeding medicine exclusively, I wanted to be among them. I found the specialty that I had been looking for way back that cares for both mother and baby as a unit. In addition to maintaining my Primary Board Certification in Family Medicine, I chose to further my education by becoming an International Board Certified Lactation Consultant (IBCLC).

Deep down, I had hoped that I could make a lateral move within the hospital. I wanted to continue in urgent care part-time and work in maternity with new mothers the other days. To demonstrate my sincere interest and knowledge to my employer, I accepted the invitation to join the Board of Directors at the Birthing Center. I also voluntarily attended committee meetings to help the hospital achieve the highest recognition in breastfeeding a hospital can attain: "Baby-Friendly," a designation by the World Health Organization.

I really thought administration would be excited to promote the unique services I could provide as an "MD IBCLC." From an administrative perspective it would enhance their maternity department's reputation and give a competitive marketing edge.

I assumed wrong. The Birthing Center closed, and due to lack of interest from the other physicians, the Baby-Friendly committee disbanded. I easily recognized that the potential to utilize my skills as an "MD IBCLC" did not exist at this point in time in the hospital setting. Still, I was determined. I became involved in the wider community of breastfeeding medicine.

I joined the Academy of Breastfeeding Medicine and La Leche League Medical Associates. Through membership in these professional organizations, I gained 24/7 online access to breastfeeding experts around the world. I could seek opinions and references quickly for special situations.

At first, my focus was on breastfeeding support and education, but over time I became interested in how birth management affects breastfeeding. For instance, now I understood that the medication a laboring woman receives also gets to the baby. The drug's influence may inhibit the baby's natural rooting reflex and contribute to a poor start at feeding. Perineal soreness and cesarean incision site pain interfere with the ability to sit in an ideal position to breastfeed. Even having an IV needle in place can interfere with how a mom holds and positions her baby. These are just a few of many ways that interference can cause mothers to give up breastfeeding before they've had a chance to find out how good breastfeeding can be.

Understanding how breastfeeding works brought me back to being involved with birth. I wasn't in a practice situation where I could provide prenatal care and actually deliver babies. But I knew I could feel good about incorporating my newly acquired skills in breastfeeding medicine and let the doulas concentrate on the births.

MY FRIEND'S SURPRISE HOMEBIRTH

I felt psyched about finally knowing how to help women have better birth experiences. I wanted to tell every pregnant woman about what a difference it makes to have a doula. Being in contact with so many families as a physician in the urgent care center, I thought I'd be a credible voice that could reach many women. I wanted so much to help women to avoid bad birth experiences.

Most pregnant women in the general population were actually quite resistant to my suggestions. Joan, however, took everything I said to heart. I met Joan at La Leche League meetings during her first trimester. She was preparing early for her birth. She spent a lot of time outside surfing and gardening. In touch with nature, she was committed to natural birth.

Joan received prenatal care from an obstetrician. Even though she wanted a natural birth, she also wanted to birth at the hospital. Joan was older (38), this was a first-time baby, and she had a history of abdominal surgery and post-op scarring after an automobile accident 20 years earlier. At our meetings there was a lot of talk about "wonderful" homebirths, but Joan remained convinced that a homebirth wasn't for her. Still she transferred her plan to birth at the birth center. All our group meetings were held there, and she felt comfortable hanging out there. She decided it was the next best thing to home.

I scared Joan to death with my honesty. Not intentionally, but I told her in detail how awful my first labor was and how most first time moms have long painful 24-hour labors. I told her how sore she'd be for days.

I told her about my first night home with my oldest son. He woke crying and hungry, but I had to use the bathroom badly. I got out of bed and gushed blood on our white carpet. With a full bladder, pain and bleeding, a stained carpet, an upset husband and a crying baby, I didn't know what to do first. She had stairs, and I didn't know how she'd do it, I said.

The more I scared her, the more Joan was motivated to prepare and network and read up on the birth experience. I was so excited to talk to someone who was preparing for birth so early in her pregnancy. Joan was equally excited to hear all that

I had to offer. She was one of the first women I was able to persuade to have a doula. She hired her doula early on, almost as soon as I told her about mine. She didn't give me a hundred reasons why she didn't think she needed one.

I am not sure why I waited until 32 weeks to start calling for a doula. For me it worked out fine, but you can never be too prepared, especially for the first labor. Joan was doing all the things I could have done with my first pregnancy.

All of Joan's preparations paid off. Her contractions weren't intense at all. Her waters broke when she was outside watering the garden. All in all the labor lasted 1 ½ hours, and only two of the contractions made her want to howl. She didn't push except once when she thought she had to use the toilet. That's when her baby slipped out of her like a baby giraffe. Her doula arrived soon after.

I was working at urgent care that day. Joan called me to ask what to do with her baby. Could she bring the baby to me for the first check-up? I was longing to get my hands on that baby and give her baby a clearance of good health. But how do you clear a baby that was born at home? Besides, the urgent care was never used for newborn assessment before. Would I get reprimanded by the powers that be for doing something like that?

As much as I wanted to say yes to examining Joan's baby, I told her to relax with her baby and provide skin-to-skin. After they had a good nursing session, go to the birth center to be checked out. Even if I got away with checking the baby, how would I explain why I was "finishing a birth" at the urgent care?

The only negative or upsetting event from her birth was that she was criticized of planning things that way. It made me wish I had accepted her to the urgent care.

I finally got my hands on that baby a few days later, when I went to Joan's house to help her with breastfeeding. Her home décor was so relaxed, with hammocks in her house, the beauty of her garden, the view of the canal and her surfboards. I wondered if maybe she was so in tune with nature that it brought about an easy birth.

Now I was the personal friend of someone who was birth-wise and had had an unassisted homebirth. In fact, I was almost an accomplice in this case! I had become an eccentric by association! Furthermore, I realized I had come close to having a medically unassisted birth with Scott. I had been only a few contractions away from having him at home, and it wouldn't have been the worst thing in the world.

HEALTHIER IMAGES OF PREGNANCY

Our local breastfeeding community was thriving, and so was Gentle Spirit Doulas. This is a support group for women providing doula services founded by my doula Bernadette. The group publishes *Mother to Mother (M2M)*, a quarterly birth and breastfeeding journal for parents and their health care providers. Through doula-attended birth stories, *M2M's* goal is to restore Godly confidence to women in their ability to birth their own babies. I had been a captive reader.

Bernadette asked me to write my birth story for *Mother to Mother*. Can you imagine that I resisted and exaggerated? "I can't write, I can't type, and I don't know Microsoft Word! And I don't have time." Finally, I grudgingly agreed to write the story, "but only if you proofread it."

As it turns out, I enjoyed the whole process of writing about my births. I found another aspect of personal growth through the writing and editing process. Women tend to like telling their birth stories, and I was especially excited to have a new way to promote the doulas' purpose. I recommend that every woman have a doula whether birthing in a hospital, birth center or home.

I was also getting to know the doula group through other mutual projects. Several pregnant doulas gave me an opportunity to combine my interest in photography and pregnancy with some casual photo shoots of them late in pregnancy. I learned a lot.

These doulas viewed themselves as beautiful in pregnancy. I had been through two pregnancies and felt big and frumpy. My sister took some token pictures of me when I was pregnant that I never intended to show anyone. My negative self-image limited her artistic skills. I was intrigued how my new doula friends viewed themselves and their pregnancy shapes. It seemed I couldn't take a bad picture of any of them. These women were so comfortable in their own skin and confident about their changing shapes that they were uninhibited in photographs and empowered in their births.

After the breastfeeding meetings were adjourned, the "after-meeting" in the parking lot was often about homebirth. Several League moms and doulas shared their loving homebirth stories and photos. These were very different from any hospital birth I had experienced, either personally or professionally.

I came to use many of these photos to decorate the breastfeeding rooms in my medical practice. I want other women to see pregnancy in this beautiful light. I want child-bearing aged women to feel safe in my exam room. I couldn't help but think back to the rooms at my OB's office that were decorated with posters and adverts for trendy cosmetic procedures. During pregnancy those posters just served as a constant nine-month campaign that said I should be ashamed of my natural self. It made me feel like my safe birth wasn't as important to them as their aesthetic clientele. I should be more concerned with my bikini line, stretch marks and varicose veins, the posters said, than with my primordial mothering instincts to emerge.

My social circle increasingly included mothers who were planning midwife-attended births at home or at the birth center. A small part of me (the medically trained part) wanted to reject the idea that homebirths were a safe choice. Another part of me wanted to know more, more, more.

My mind was so polluted with unhealthy images of hospital birth from my previous employment, training, and mainstream television. These snapshots would flash through my mind as if to frighten me away from considering homebirth. Then I had the opportunity to watch a few videos of gentle water births, which the families involved described as the birth of their dreams. Viewing these important life events expanded my horizons and helped replace in my mind the memories of traumatic hospital births.

BERNADETTE'S 11TH BLESSING

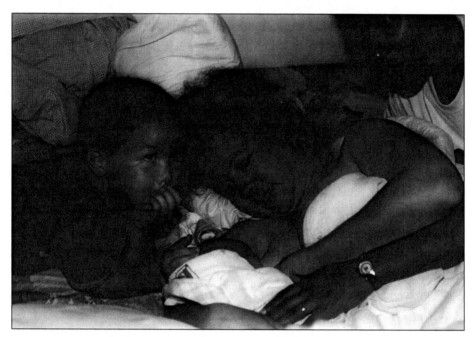

My photography career/hobby was at its peak. Bernadette welcomed me and my camera to the birth of her 11th blessing. It amuses me to realize that in inviting me to her birth, she was still "doula-ing" me. She was still helping to create a complete shift in the way I viewed birth.

I was already at least halfway there due to the stories and videos my friends had shared with me. In fact, I may have already been convinced. But there is nothing like being witness to a baby's birth at home. What I learned from this experience would shape my next birth and affect all the women who I have counseled ever since.

As Bernadette's due date approached I wondered if I would even make it to the birth. I was reminded of how taxing it could be to be on call for one birth. Physicians usually take turns being on call and deliver whoever happens to show up on their call night. Typically, if a physician wants to deliver a particular woman's baby, he does it by inducing the woman when it's convenient for him. The doulas and midwives who make commitments to a specific client to be at her birth have my utmost respect.

Bernadette told me that she was in no rush and that she usually goes past her due date. She explained that her baby was in the safest place, "We are too anxious to see what G-d is still creating in that secret place. He barely gets to put on the finishing touches before we snatch the baby from the womb." Her seventh homebirth was her longest wait, going to 20 days past the due date.

When Bernadette finally called me to tell me she was in labor, I was trapped at work for two more hours and faced a 40-minute drive on top of that. I assumed she would deliver in that time frame, and I couldn't believe that colds and flu were going to interfere with me being present at an amazing birth.

When I got to her house, two of Bernadette's kids were outside playing with pogo sticks like on any ordinary day. Busy having fun, they couldn't tell me whether the birth had already occurred: they didn't know! Most of the ten kids were just hanging out. I noticed an overwhelmingly peaceful atmosphere. Bernadette had two doulas, her husband, a midwife and another friend with her. All were very special people and had a place in this celebration. How many women birthing in the hospital can claim that everyone present was praying for them? Here, love and prayer was plentiful.

As for a focal point, I noticed the Scriptures posted on the wall, over the bed, opposite the toilet, on the fridge, anywhere your eye might rest. Still a novelty to me, this beat having the distraction of a clock, a medical poster, or a roommates TV to stare at. Now, there were *some* births in residency with prayer and low intervention, with attending physicians sensitive to this need. But there were not enough of those births to balance out the highly interventional births etched in my mind.

I never met either of Bernadette's doulas before, but I felt connected to them in purpose this day. I have stayed in touch with them through their next births and pregnancy losses. As it turned out, the baby was born before I arrived, but the peacefulness of this homebirth made an impression on me. It left me wondering how birth ever strayed so far from home.

In residency we were taught that a grand-multip (a medical label for a woman who has had many births) just "spits them out." But here, I did not get the impression that Bernadette just spit them out. I understood at a very deep level that there are couples that desire large families, who plan and pray for their well-being and the baby's, and that each of their birthing experiences and children are unique.

I enjoyed photographing the postpartum activities, the support Bernadette was receiving and her nursing the new baby. I really enjoyed watching how the older siblings then took turns loving and holding the newborn. They were not shunned. I realized that's how it should be: a newly-arrived baby should have the pleasure of being welcomed by its family, not on a nursery warming table getting poked and prodded or lined up at the viewing window.

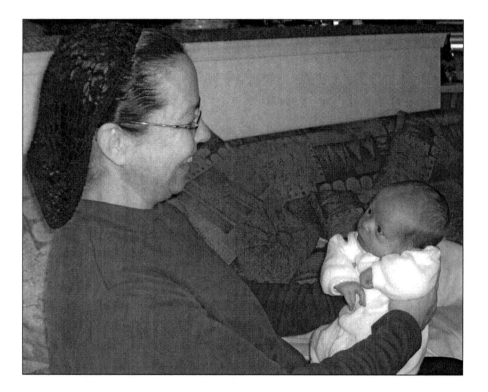

Another difference was the way the placenta was dealt with. At Bernadette's birth, we let the placenta deliver in its own time and took time to observe it as an organ of life, not something gross that belongs to the pathology lab. The older kids were fascinated by it.

Finally, I was impressed with the pizza. At a homebirth you can eat pizza as soon as you want after giving birth. What a great way to recharge and get your energy back.

What an honor is was to be with my doula and her family during such as special time. And how inspiring to watch what came next. Bernadette bounced back full of life, busy with all the kids' activities and working towards her R.N. degree. She had her 12th baby three years later. What an encouragement to women still having babies in their forties.

ANOTHER MISSED HOMEBIRTH

For a time, my family and I moved to Georgia. I found a group of birthing and breastfeeding friends there. One evening, at a moms' meeting, I took a few spontaneous photos of a near-term woman with her two-year-old hugging her belly. I dropped the photos off at her house a week later. She loved them, and I was glad I could give her the photos as a token of this pregnancy. She was feeling a little "crampy" that day, she said, but she rested comfortably. A mutual friend, Doula Dora, was giving her a massage. I thought how nice of the doula to give this much attention to a pregnant woman not yet in labor.

Two short hours after I left, the subject of those photos delivered at home with Doula Dora and a local midwife in attendance. I secretly pouted that I had missed another homebirth. If only I had recognized the contractions, I surely could have come up with a way to put off my departure and bring my camera back out. As it was, I was apparently doomed just to see beginnings and endings of homebirths.

In residency, the babies that counted were the ones I could record in my procedure log after I delivered them. I didn't know back then that there was a lot to learn even from just the beginnings and endings. Many OBs don't bother with a laboring woman until she is ready to deliver. They rely on the nurses for reports. I thought of the faculty members who had always been on the lookout for disease: *They missed all the joy of being in a privileged profession like obstetrics.* Now, Dora was holding this new baby and saying, "How can you look at a baby and not know this is a gift from God." I never really thought of it this way.

There was another mother in our small group who had a stillbirth a few months later. Dora helped me see the meaning in that sad event, too. "The stillbirth," she told the group, "is a reminder that life is fragile and can change in an instant.

GETTING READY FOR MY OWN HOMEBIRTH

After Scott's birth, I really didn't think I would have another baby. I had my two healthy sons, so by cultural standards it was time to stop. To my own satisfaction, I had my healing birth. To my husband's pleasure, I had steady income.

There is five years between Scott and my next son, David. I'm glad I wasn't stuck in the mold that two kids are enough.

At the time, John and I weren't sure if moving to Georgia was a permanent or temporary decision. So we came back to Florida quarterly to keep our professional options open. John was employed in Georgia. As for me, I postponed any new employment. It was a good time to have another baby.

Like my first pregnancies, I had a conscious conception once again. The first visit back to Florida, I knew it was day 14. Bernadette and her teens very conveniently cared for my kids

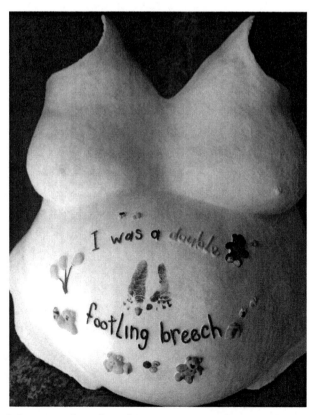

at her house that evening. When John saw the plus sign on my pregnancy test two

47

weeks later, he called it a conspiracy with my more fertile friend.

I already knew my birth plan. This time, I would give birth surrounded by a midwife and my doula friends in the comfort of my own home.

As soon as I knew I was pregnant, I sent e-mail to my doula friends in Florida. Their initial replies were exciting; I felt so special. Through e-mail, a listserv, and instant messaging, it was so easy to stay in touch. Although I was far away I could still talk to my birthing friends almost daily online. Early on, my doulas joked via e-mail that they would caravan to my birth. My husband reminded me it was just a joke, but I obliged them to follow through by taking their offer seriously.

Scott's birth left me fully confident that I could birth without intervention. The homebirths I had experienced (even just the beginnings and endings) further reinforced my trust in my body. Articles in *Mother to Mother* imprinted on my heart the knowledge that if I ever had another baby, its birth would be a time of enormous personal growth. Although I believed another birth would be positively life-altering, I had no idea how and to what extent. My second birth had been empowering, and it was hard to imagine it getting any better.

Still, there were a few things I did want to avoid this time. I didn't want to experience the transition phase of labor in the car. I wanted to embrace each and *every* contraction with all physical, emotional, and spiritual support available to me via my doula. I didn't want to be distracted by the logistics of getting to the hospital.

I could have been spared that tearing had I been allowed to follow my instinct and semi-squat. Squatting naturally opens our pelvis outlet. Conversely, being on your back the way women do in most hospital births is restrictive and usually anti-intuitive.

Also, I wanted to surround myself with positive providers at delivery. The female OB who told me to stop nursing also considered my beautiful, totally natural and empowering birth "complicated." Why? Because I labored at home unmonitored. Because she wasn't right there, this birth was labeled "precipitous." Because my nine pound baby was big. Because I had torn on the outside. I wanted to avoid the invasive postpartum check for cervical tears, but because of my "complicated" birth she had her hand up in me, checking for internal tears while I was just about coming off the bed in pain. I wanted to avoid going through that again.

In preparation for another birth, I questioned my doulas about whether this internal exam was routinely done. Fortunately, they re-assured me that in our local birth community (hospital and home) they rarely saw this done. That was great news for me and my next birth. I want to encourage birthing women not only to consider their birth plans, but also the postpartum protocols of their potential providers.

I didn't want anyone to take my baby away to a nursery. I wanted no loss time bonding with my next baby. To meet my needs it made sense to birth at home. I knew from Scott's birth that I could labor without a hospital's help. And in the privacy of my home, no one would think to separate my baby from me.

Whenever anything happened in the course of this third pregnancy, John's response was, "That's it! You're getting an OB." But his demands were not going to work this time.

I often speak to women who opt not to have a homebirth because someone doesn't support that decision—their husbands, mothers, in-laws, you name it. If you are going to wait for everyone's support, you'll wait forever. If having a homebirth is important to you, you have to be the one to make the choice. Don't ask your partner, "Do you think I should interview a midwife?" Instead, say, "My appointment with the midwife is on Monday." Then go on Monday.

Of course, it's not only family members that might present an obstacle to birthing away from the hospital. Another reason I often hear is that insurance won't cover it. But don't assume that. In many cases, insurance *does* cover other birth options. Research and ask questions. But don't assume that a service is not valuable if it's not a covered benefit.

Women in my local cesarean support group, International Cesarean Awareness Network, have concluded that what causes a cesarean is not necessarily a last minute emergency in the middle of labor. Rather, a cesarean is the result of a cascade of events that begins with the kind of healthcare provider a woman chooses. That decision, in many cases, is being based on a referral from insurance companies. A referral solely from an insurance company is not an informed choice. It's worth it to go out-of-network, if that means finding a provider that can meet your needs.

We are talking about your birth, your baby, your welfare. The decisions you make early on will affect you throughout the pregnancy. Carefully research your choices of provider and options. The leader of our cesarean support group has had two vaginal hospital births after two cesareans. Nothing is impossible!

~♥~

Throughout my third pregnancy I was quite involved with the production of *Mother to Mother*. I had been promoted to medical editor and was contributing my articles and photos on a regular basis. (Yes, I get a kick out of the fact that I didn't want to write my story, but once I started I've never stopped.) Working on *M2M* was a great way to give back to the community that gave me so much support.

You see, I am somewhat "high maintenance" when it comes to pregnancy. I don't need much medical attention, but I do need interpersonal support. I need someone who will share the experience with me, who will hear me out on everything I am doing and feeling, who will reply with encouragement. My birthing and breastfeeding community gave me all that and more, so I was happy to return the favor.

It was a great experience to edit *Mother to Mother* while I was pregnant. All the stories were refreshing, optimistic and spiritual. Reading these positive stories so closely during the editing process provided the reassurance I needed. Ever have anyone tell you her nightmare horror story about being pregnant and birthing? That is not what I wanted to hear while I was mentally preparing to labor. The articles in *Mother to Mother* were so good for me.

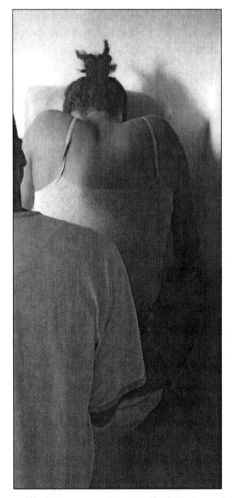

I've read a few "empty" birth stories on-line where the "ability" to hire a doula comes across more or less a status symbol or a quick-fix for the birthing woman. That attitude does not necessarily lead to successful birth outcomes. The story-line is equivalent to a timetable of medical interventions. I liked the doula-attended birth stories in the *M2M* articles that emphasize personal growth and insight.

Mother to Mother includes educational articles, also. One informative piece I edited was about chiropractic techniques for turning a breech. A breech is a baby who is positioned to come out feet first or rump first. Coming out vertex (head first) is the "acceptable" way. I had never studied chiropractic techniques very much, so I did a review of this before approving the article. I was surprised to find out there were many natural ways to attempt to turn a breech.

In fact, I was surprised to realize that a breech was such a big deal. In my training, the way you dealt with a breech baby was pretty simple: you cut him out with a c-section. More recently I have learned that while some OBs will do a procedure called External Version, an attempt to turn the baby; some OBs won't, citing a repertoire of risks (low fluid, long cord) that outweigh the benefit of turning and/or they may trivialize the risks of the inevitable cesarean.

Chiropractors relax and realign a mother's muscles and spine to encourage the baby to turn on its own. This is called the Webster technique, and it's just one of many techniques that people have used successfully. What sounds safer, scheduling a cesarean or trying natural attempts to turn a baby? Why won't obstetricians encourage women to try these techniques? Does it go back to their surgical mindset that they are the only ones that can cure? What holds women back from seeking other opinions? If it were me and it came down to surgery versus trying a natural and safe, technique to avoid the risks of surgery, do I have anything to lose?

While I was absorbing this new information, I was rubbing my big pregnant belly, *sure my baby was vertex* and glad I didn't have to worry about a breech.

In addition to *Mother to Mother*, I also spent this pregnancy reading encouraging words from midwives. My favorite resources were *Ina Mae's Guide to Childbirth*, *Motherwit*, *Baby Catcher*, *Birthing from Within* and *Midwifery Today*.

Why is it important to read stories of hope? Because we are surrounded by the horror stories of everything that can go wrong. Talk shows and daytime soap operas are based on fear. And tragedy makes "good" television. These stories create a sense of powerlessness in women. By contrast, the anthologies I read were written by midwives who respect the birth rights of women.

Back when I was helping Jayne as a resident, and even later when I hired a doula before delivering my second baby, I couldn't visualize a birth where the laboring woman was in control. Jayne and I were very similar, actually: The only way we knew to stay in charge of our birthing was to put off coming to the hospital as long as possible. Before these events, I had never seen a woman be in charge of her own labor. No one had modeled that for me, so I could not offer it to Jayne. I didn't know that I could have insisted that the nurses leave her alone and let her birth in her own way.

Today, I strongly encourage women to read and watch videos of empowering birth stories. Read and watch a lot of them. These will introduce you to other possibilities for your own birth experience.

If you don't know what I mean about what TV images do to our minds, here is an example. The Rugrats were popular during my third pregnancy. My 5- and 6-year-old sons seemed to find one particular episode over and over: It was the one in which one of the moms was having a baby. My boys saw the Rugrats mom in a wheel chair when it was time to birth her baby and thought something was wrong. "Mom, are you going to need a wheel chair, too?"

My sons associate wheel chairs with being ill or disabled in some way. Who doesn't? The image of a wheel chair even in cartoons embeds fear. I was glad I could reassure them that at our homebirth I wouldn't need a wheel chair. Giving birth is not a sickness or a handicap. I don't want to be in a sick role or anything that mimics helplessness.

Because the image of birth as a sickness is everywhere in our culture, I actively focused on giving my boys a positive image of birth. I showed them the photos that I took right after my doula's homebirth. They looked at the baby's picture and asked, "When does she get a name (hospital) bracelet?" I explained that there is no risk of switching babies at home, so she didn't need a band.

Another time, I showed the boys an anatomically correct mother doll with a baby. I put

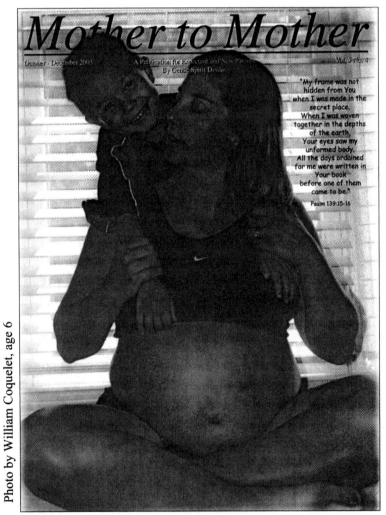

Photo by William Coquelet, age 6

the baby doll in the mama doll's belly and showed them what a baby looks like coming out. I told them that during our homebirth, they would be able to see our baby's head emerge. I gave them the "job" of telling me if there was hair and what color it was as soon as they saw it. They were excited that they would be able to touch the baby's head, and they were full of questions. "Can a baby come out sideways or feet first?"

I also read "new baby" books to my boys that illustrated natural birth and feedings without bottles. I knew they were beginning to understand when my older son touched my heart and asked, "Why wasn't I born at home?" All I could say was that I didn't know better at the time.

William had another question for me. "Why did you have me if it hurts?"

I told him, "Because the pain is just for a few hours, then I get to love you for years and years."

When I shared this conversation with my doula Bernadette, I learned that she identifies with the sacrificial aspects of her religion to help her get through the pain of childbirth. "What a powerful meditation that is for Christian women," I thought. I had always liked how *Mother to Mother's* readers were encouraged to seek a spiritual side of birth. Now I could appreciate the spiritual facet of *M2M* even more.

My own religious heritage is Jewish, so I had to go beyond *M2M* to explore what the spirituality of childbirth meant to me. I also wanted to know what Jewish woman were meditating on during birth. I searched thoroughly. Most Torah-based searches lead me to the *Simchat Bat* and *Bris*. That is a celebration of the baby, but not the process of birth itself. Eventually, I found a meditation at JewishPregnancy.org and incorporated it into my birth plan. While writing this book, I also found another resource for Jewish woman at miriammaslin.com. I haven't yet found a Jewish publication similar to *Mother to Mother* that emphasizes the spiritual aspect of birth.

Creativity is a major way that I express the spirituality of pregnancy and birth. Enjoying my artistic channels kept me focused on the beauty of pregnancy.

There was the photography, of course. I had often taken photos of women who were slender when they got pregnant and were all belly when they were at the end of pregnancy. This time, I was nearly 200 pounds when I became pregnant and assumed I'd gain 50 pounds like I had with my other pregnancies. I didn't think I'd be very photogenic.

But I was wrong. It all turned into baby. I didn't gain that much this pregnancy, and I love my pregnancy photos. My all-time favorite photos of myself were taken during this pregnancy. One was even on the cover of *Mother to Mother*! This represented a big change in my self-perception: I never wanted my picture taken during my earlier pregnancies. During this one, my photographers were my sons and my sister. And they all did a good job!

In addition to the photography, I got into some sculpting. I made two belly casts this pregnancy. My sons asked why I needed a cast. Did I break my belly?

I made the first cast while visiting my sister in Seattle at 28 weeks. Making it with her was a lot of fun, but trying to get the delicate sculpture home was not. I knew it wouldn't make it through an airport and flight. I went into a pack-n-ship with my belly and breast cast. I handed it to a team of young men who carefully wrapped and packed for about $80.

My doula made my second cast while I was in labor. Making a belly image is a feel good thing. It kept me focused on the beautiful growing baby inside of me. As artist Dorian of Pregnancy Memory Sculpture LLC says, "It's a declaration to [my] child of the pride [I] felt when we were one."

Along with all my artwork, I surrounded myself with pictures of my supportive friends. I wanted constant good vibes with me, especially since they were a long way away. I didn't think they would be able to come to my birth. I really didn't.

Several people suggested that I look into planning an unassisted birth because I came so close with Scott. They mistakenly assumed that this was a reasonable idea because my husband and I are physicians. I really wanted my upcoming birth to be one that I shared, not hide in isolation. Besides, I'd believed that women who had planned unassisted births often had above-average-supportive partners. My husband and I mutually agreed that he does not fit this description, at least, not when it comes to birth.

If I was alone for a long labor, who would help me change positions, take photos, watch my other children, explain to my children what was going on, handle the phone calls, get snacks, help clean up, do laundry and comfort me? I certainly could not do all that. A planned unassisted birth was not for me. I wanted a strong, social, supportive birth team.

I went along with midwifery care in Georgia. She came to my house for prenatal visits. I say "went along with" since I did not appreciate the contributions she made to my pregnancy at the time. Now I see that she had good influence that went beyond pregnancy.

For one thing, this midwife was really into nutrition and vitamins. She emphasized how important nutrition is throughout pregnancy for the developing baby and for entering labor. She strongly emphasized that entering labor with optimal nutrition is essential for normal contractions and labor progression. This made sense to me.

We eat a **SAD** diet, the **S**tandard **A**merican **D**iet. We are missing produce, fruit and grains. We eat heavily processed foods and then we feel bad, fatigued, nauseated or constipated. Then we approach labor and expect our bodies to function optimally on minimum nutrition. This midwife wanted me to be well-nourished for labor. She wanted me to take quality vitamins, whole grains and organic. Pregnancy is not a time to just barely meet our nutritional requirements.

I also learned about the late Dr. Thomas Brewer and his simple regimen of good nutrition for pregnancy. With his program, he eliminated toxemia completely from his own obstetrical practice. I was always taught that the cause of elevated blood pressure, swelling, and urine protein were unknown! Why does the medical community ignore his evidence? His balanced diet is probably how most of us should all be eating.

I was pleased to learn that this midwife didn't carry much in her birth bag in terms of herbs or emergency medicines. She said it wasn't necessary to rely on herbs and pharmaceuticals. This I liked. Even among women birthing at home, I hear so many who want to bring on their labors with cohoshes, castor oils and cervical ripeners. (See Herbal Inductions, Appendix.) To me, homebirth is all about letting Nature take its course.

The only thing I could imagine needing might be some Pitocin in case of postpartum hemorrhage. My midwife gave me several options for obtaining a prescription from homebirth-friendly family physicians.

Another good thing about this midwife was that there were fewer tests than I'd dealt with before. Midwives in Georgia couldn't order prescriptions for labs or ultrasound, because there was no licensure available to midwives in Georgia. This was all fine with me. I didn't want to get caught up into the medical system, anyway. It was my third pregnancy, and most labs don't change much from earlier pregnancies.

My midwife requested a blood count and an HIV test, but that was about all. I think all pregnant women should have an HIV test if for no other reason than to have this information available to their birth attendants.

I failed my glucose challenge tests in my first two pregnancies. Follow-up showed the results to be false positives. My early morning sugars done by accucheck were always normal. I worried that I'd "risk out" of a homebirth if I failed the challenge test this third pregnancy. She was satisfied with just following the sugars in my urine. She reassured me it was normal for my kidneys to leak some sugar into urine near the end of pregnancy. I remained within an acceptable range and I never did pull out my old accucheck machine during this pregnancy.

Birthing women gain a real advantage by having a midwife who depends on her clinical skills and wisdom rather than objective lab data. Most women need to learn to trust themselves. My last pap screen was recent, so she didn't push for any speculum or vaginal exam in my third pregnancy. I declined testing for group B streptococcus (GBS). And this was all acceptable.

My midwife from the mountains was a good hands-off clinician. She kept a good watch on my blood pressure, urine, weight and measurements. And it was also how she went about it that was non-threatening. She came to my house. We sat at my table first to get caught up, and I had a chance to ask questions. I didn't have to get on a scale in front of her. She could take my word for it. Then I went to the bathroom for the urine specimen. My blood pressure and fundal height and fetal heart tones were all checked in my bed.

This is a contrast to how my prenatal appointments went with my previous OB. A nurse calls you to the back. She directs you to the bathroom first, and then scale, and then a chair for blood pressure. Without making eye contact she gathers all your personal data (weight and urine), things we don't usually share with anyone, and puts you in a room for the OB visit. This is the room with all the ads about getting rid of unwanted lines and veins, as well as endorsements from formula and pharmaceuticals companies. This impersonal assembly line treatment alone is enough to make me not want me to go back there.

Although I incorporated only a small portion of her dietary changes while I was pregnant, I am better off for the foundation she laid. Over the years, fewer preservative, more whole grains and organics became a part of my routine diet.

So there was a lot to appreciate in my Georgia midwife, but I missed the deep connections I had in Florida. Also, I had a problem in that I did not have a local doula.

My friends in Florida continued to provide the social and interpersonal reassurance I needed, even at a distance, so I was still enjoying this pregnancy. The doulas in Florida expressed their interest in coming to me for my due date. It was so hard to believe this dream could come true. I was still going down to Florida for quarterly visits. In my last trimester, I was proud to flaunt my pregnancy around people who cared. One of my doulas, Dawn, introduced me to the midwife that delivered her last baby. Dawn encouraged her to caravan to Georgia, too.

We all got together for a meeting to work out the plans. I was with four women who made me feel I was on top of the world. I felt like my birth was going to be the most important birth they'd ever witnessed. I felt like my family and our needs were important. What a high! All childbearing women should feel this way. They were actually excited to come to me and stay with me around my due date. Their enthusiasm meant so much to me. I could be happy about this and enjoy the last months of my pregnancy, confident I'd have my team! Doula

Regena reassured me that help was on the way!

I felt like my labor wanted to start but was waiting for my birthing caravan. If only I could hang on. They arrived a week before my due date. What a relief to have a midwife and two doulas in my house! We stayed up way too late talking about my pregnancy, my birth plans, my 5- and 6-year-old sons' level of participation, my husband's role and anything related. There was so much to talk about. All this talk got my hormones going. I knew it wouldn't be long.

"IT'S TOES!"

The next morning my new midwife noticed that I had the waddle and complexion of someone in pre-labor. I didn't even tell her the Braxton Hicks contractions were getting regular! She assessed the heart tones and we went about our day. I stayed hydrated on fudge bars and chicken soup. My instant messenger was on, so I could send the updates to my friends stuck in Florida. While the contractions were still regular, we made a belly cast. The project kept me laughing.

The midwife showed William and Scott all of her midwife equipment as she set up and demonstrated on stuffed animals. They thought she was the coolest. In fact, I think her attention solidified the two older brothers' bond with their baby brother. All the while, we women discussed birth, babies and breastfeeding. The midwife talked about the various birthing scenarios she hoped never to encounter, one of which was a footling breech where the baby comes out feet first.

Throughout the day my doulas questioned if I was really in labor, because I seemed so calm and able to laugh at our jokes or what my sons were doing. Actually, I wondered if I was in labor. I had imagined laboring with a third would be much quicker. You never know.

But the most important thing was not the length of labor, but that I remained in control the whole time. After the cast was done, the contractions became more convincing. I sat on a birth ball as Dawn massaged my back. After I changed positions to the rocking chair my midwife massaged my feet and calves, emphasizing the uterine pressure points. My husband finally came home from work and he too questioned whether I was really laboring: We all seemed too peaceful to him. "We don't need a doctor to diagnose labor," my midwife told him jokingly. "The signs are unmistakable." The fact that I turned off my IM and e-mail for the first time in nine months was truly a sign of how close to birth I was.

After the foot massage, I tried side-lying in bed just to get some rest, not sure

59

how much longer I had to go. At a certain point, I did what seemed natural and sat on the side of the bed with my feet propped on a stool; it allowed me the benefit of gravity. The doulas were on either side of me, providing comforting touch.

This intuitive position turned out to be critical. Since I was upright, no one could be peaking in my bottom seeing what "surprise" was coming. And there would be no premature panicking over the presenting part.

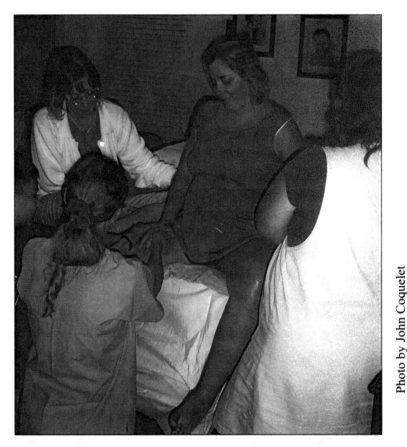

Photo by John Coquelet

Sitting there, I suddenly felt my waters burst. At the same time the phone rang. Who could be calling now?

One of the doulas took the call. It was Bernadette back in Florida, calling to send a prayer and tell me she couldn't sleep until she knew that this baby was born and we were all well. The call meant a lot to me, and the fact that it came at the same time that my membranes ruptured didn't seem like a coincidence to me!

I kept looking for signs that my body was reaching transition. I visualized the baby's head coming down, my cervix opening and the kind of sensations I would have in my perineum. But I didn't have those familiar feelings from my previous pregnancies. I felt like reaching down to see if I could feel the baby's head, but I didn't do it. I wanted to ask my team if they saw a head, but then I thought it would be too discouraging if they said no. Instead, I kept visualizing the head crowning.

All of a sudden I had a strange sensation in my vagina. "Something's coming out," I announced. I thought it was a huge clot. It certainly was not a head crowning. My midwife and doulas repositioned me to my back to look. That's when my six-year-old William exclaimed, "It's toes!"

Toes? How could that be? So many sets of hands had been on my abdomen from several midwives, physician friends and doulas. The baby was vertex. There was no doubt. When did this baby flip? Then I recalled slipping on a wet floor in my bathroom about a week before. I had been stunned and sore. Could that have turned my baby?

As I thought of different scenarios, I saw my life flash before me. Had this last minute discovery of a double footling breech occurred in a hospital, I would have had an anesthesia mask slapped on my face to put me to sleep and then been whisked to surgery to have my abdomen and uterus barbarically cut open to rescue my breech. On the other hand, had I let my quick labor progress at home without an experienced midwife present, I might have lost my life, my son's life or both.

My midwife said later that my birth required skillful maneuvering (posterior rotation and flexion at the neck) to prevent the chin from getting stuck in the pubic ring. I sensed the confidence of my midwife to handle the situation. My doula Regena who read up about the hands-off approach to breech birth later confirmed that David resisted an optimal position and needed to be turned. I also noticed my midwife was able to keep John, my doctor husband, calm. Both of these things gave me the strength I needed.

I was determined to push my baby out on the next contraction. I thought I only had a few minutes to give a grand-finale type push with all my might before my baby would be compromised. On the next two successive contractions, I wailed without holding anything back and pushed with every bit of energy I could muster. What a relief it was to feel my baby's body slip out and to hear him cry!

My midwife remained composed and confident as she adjusted her plan and safely delivered my son. She observed his purple legs (that were also black and blue) and as a precaution immediately gave him three puffs of mouth-to-mouth resuscitation. David turned pink all over, and she placed him on my chest. (I later learned that his purple color was normal. It's the color our babies are when they're inside the womb. Usually, though, they come out head first and get oxygen into their little bodies before we see the purple feet.)

I examined David's ears and spine to eliminate any concern over Down syndrome and Spina bifida. I'd had an abnormal triple screen earlier in my pregnancy (the one test I regrettably had to please my husband) and opted not to have an ultrasound or amniocentesis, knowing I wanted this baby no matter what. Seeing he was healthy, I felt a wave of relief.

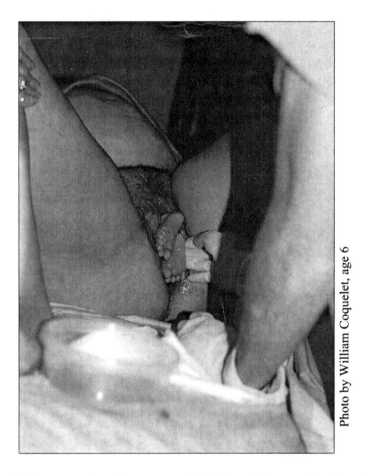

Photo by William Coquelet, age 6

Few midwives or physicians can skillfully deliver a footling breech without complications. The dangers include cord compression or prolapse, one or two broken arms, palsy or even stillbirth. All we had to deal with were two bruised legs and a cephalohematoma, which is a blood-filled tumor or swelling beneath the scalp that resolves by itself, generally caused by birth trauma. I even discovered an unexpected advantage of breech birth: Two curious, wide-open, brown eyes greeted us. David's eyes weren't swollen shut from head compression like my other babies' had been. He was just as curious to meet us as we were to meet him.

I brought him to my breast. John got to cut David's cord. He made a toast about how William and Scott were *still* attached by the cord, and he wanted to make sure the cord was cut this time. My midwife weighed David, who weighed nine pounds even, just like both of his brothers did. She thoughtfully delayed examining my perineum while we celebrated. I was intact: Even though I ended up on my back for the last push. No stitches required. Now I was free to eat my celebratory pizza in bed.

My older boys were totally engrossed in the miracle of birth. I attribute that to the preparation I gave them, but also to my birth team. William took my favorite photograph of my labor: David's feet emerging from me. All the other cameras missed this shot, but William's four-foot stature gave him the perfect view. At only six years old, he had the common sense to capture this once-in-a-lifetime event. I can't imagine many other birth practitioners letting a young boy be as involved as mine was. Both older brothers couldn't wait to hold David. William especially treated him like he was his own baby. What a joy to see! What an experience to have my family and friends in my own home to share this special birth and bonding time.

The midwife and both doulas stayed with me for three days after the birth. I had never heard of a midwife willing to travel so far and sleep in a child's top bunk, not even knowing when labor might occur. These five days were like a modern day "red tent," a place where women celebrate the cycles of life while sharing secrets and friendship. (See Anita Diamant's book, *The Red Tent*.) I doubt that I could have labored so uninhibitedly if there had been anyone present that didn't have total trust in the natural process of birth.

My midwife has since said that David's birth was quite an experience for her. "As the days have passed, I am awed at David's journey. I will hang in my office, like a trophy, the picture of his tiny purple feet standing outside of his warm wet world," she said. "I am honored that God would gift me with this awesome experience. But, I am also saddened that so few practitioners will ever stand at the foot of a woman's bed and watch with surprise as two tiny feet emerge over the perineum."

I am proud to have delivered my double footling breech baby in the safety of my own home on September 12, 2003 around 11:10 p.m. May my son David go through life always landing on his feet first.

A LETTER TO MY THIRD SON

David, I gaze into your inquisitive eyes. You're so curious about your family and the world brand new to you. I smell your skin so clean and pure, not even bathed yet. I count your tiny little fingers and toes. How precious to be you. I am in awe of your vulnerability, so totally dependent on me. I marvel at your birth and all the love and fulfillment that has come my way because of you. You are only two days old.

I wonder if I'll ever be able to put you down. I wonder if you will feel this way when you have your own baby. I long that this cherished moment never ends, just me and you, my David, laying together in our space—the place where you were born in our home with no one to interfere with our early moments.

What was it like for me when I was two days old? Grandma was given "twilight" that knocked her out for my

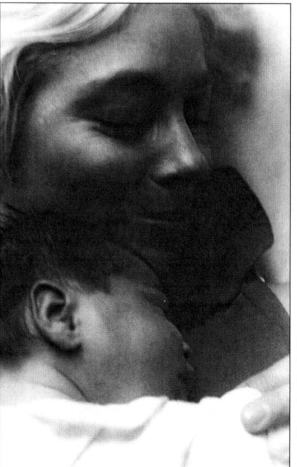

Photo by Carrie Thompson

birth and later for my sister's. She doesn't know. She doesn't know what birth can be.

David, does she even have memories of bonding with her newborn, with me? She was still drugged out from the labor meds forced upon her during an induction of convenience. Her obstetrician of choice was on call that day, she has told me, which was one reason they picked that day. The other reason was that by planning my birthday she could in turn plan a *bris*, in case I was a boy. Ours was a secular Jewish household and she didn't know my sex, yet such weight was placed onto where the eighth day would fall. I can't figure that. Breastfeeding was never mentioned to her. I never had one drop of breastmilk. As a result of the iatrogenic interference during my birth (and artificial feeds), I had jaundice requiring phototherapy and an exchange blood transfusion. While I was in the nursery, she missed out on this priceless time we share in this moment.

I didn't get the bonding time I needed as a dependent newborn. She was just a baby, too, a vulnerable 18 year old. No one gave her birth and feeding choices.

David, you are so lucky. I know now to follow my instincts. I know my options. I am fortunate to be in circumstances that gave me the opportunity to be informed and allow me to make my own decisions. Thirty-eight years later, her birth experience still affects me. What I choose now will influence you forever.

THE "AWESOME AND POWERFUL" EXPERIENCE OF RUMPING

E veryone asks, "Were you nervous about him being breech?" I worried a full nine months over whether my doulas would attend my birth, but for only *two minutes* of my entire pregnancy was I aware of David Stuart's breech presentation. What an impact these last minutes made!

Throughout my pregnancy, my preparation to birth vaginally included imagery of "the awesome and powerful sensation of crowning." My visualizations included affirmations that I *can* do this, the position in which I anticipated pushing and the feelings of being close to those I love. I decorated my room with birth-related trinkets to remind me of caring family and friends. *And* I put forth effort praying for an awareness of a Divine presence while crowning. Crowning, the part of birth when my baby would be between two worlds; what an incredible place to be! A time in our lives, rivaling with dying, that we should feel especially close to G-d. I wanted to savor this short time I'd be in labor.

I chose a meditation to memorize and recite that would give me a focal point to concentrate on while pushing. I focused on the four letters of G-d's most sacred name in Hebrew. One letter represents the head and wisdom, another represents the face, the next letter the body and the final letter the womb, symbolizing opening.

After my first birth I wished I had been more mentally fit, as non-productive, disorganized contractions fill my entire body without any urge to push. My second birth caught me pleasantly by surprise; *a great and mighty, cooperative, external force* captured my attention and guided this birth. My baby's descent couldn't be held back! During my third delivery I wanted to recognize and treasure this feeling and completely surrender to its power. And I did!

I tried to experience every physical and spiritual sensation of crowning, as I had rehearsed. Being at home, I would do this without being shaved, prepped, injected, cut or transported by car or gurney. The unrehearsed surprise of my son's breech presentation added a twist, or was this the Reward for all my preparation? Because of my imagery, the labor forces were strong, and my awareness of the physical signs of impending birth contributed to an efficient delivery. I was able to push successfully, without inhibition.

When I announced David's birth to my roommate from med school, she reminisced that I had called her after William's birth to tell her birth was the most awful experience. She was due a month after me. Despite me, she did well with her son's birth, then a daughter, then vaginal twins, all in four years. I forgot that I had shared with her like that. I have come a long way.

When I told my father-in-law, a retired obstetrician, about his grandson's grand arrival, he told me, "I used to deliver footling breech babies, but an obstetrician at my [Ivy League] residency decapitated a baby. They stopped delivering breech vaginally."

Intrigued to know why, I found results of a study conducted in 2000 known as the Term Breech Trial concluding that breech babies born by elective cesarean resulted in fewer complications for both mother and baby than born vaginally. Despite ACOG's (the professional society for obstetricians and gynecologists) follow-up recommendation that all breech babies should be delivered by cesarean, around the world, midwives are still delivering breeches. I read a story in *Midwifery Today* about a midwife who planned to attend a known double footling breech. Kudos to him! My training as a physician would have made me decline a vaginal birth had I known ahead of time that David was breech. However, I have now been empowered by my "culturally unacceptable birth." I continue to read on the topic and found a more recent analysis shows no difference in outcome between vaginal and abdominal deliveries of breech babies.

Women who find out through ultrasound that their baby is breech worry for the rest of the pregnancy how to turn that baby or fear the threat of a cesarean. Few providers, especially in America, will deliver a breech. If I found out again I was carrying a breech, I'd focus my affirmations on "the awesome and powerful experience of rumping (bottom first)." I don't think I would spend very much energy on breech-turning techniques, nor would I surrender to surgery.

I suffered no postpartum depression as a result of this natural birth. My baby, David Stuart, is happy, smiling, crawling, cruising and exclusively breastfed at seven months. I attribute our good start to prenatal preparation and my supportive birth team. David Stuart snuggles in my arms, sleeping and intermittently suckling at my left breast, the side closest to my heart. I marvel in wonder at all three of my sons and their births.

THE COST OF A DOULA

Let's look at the all-too-common assumption that a pregnant mother can't afford a doula unless she's wealthy.

I greeted Stacey with her 9-day-old infant who had come to me for an initial breastfeeding consult. "Mary was your doula?" I asked.

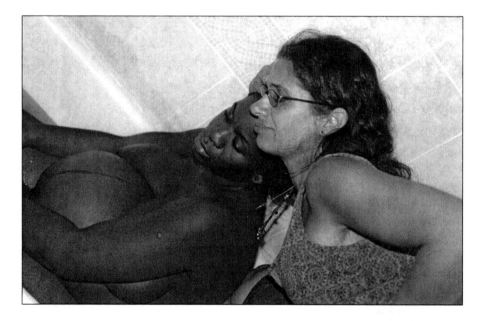

"Oh, I wish. My breastfeeding is not going well and I didn't have the birth I hoped for. I met Mary at a local crisis pregnancy center. She taught a class there."

"Tell me about your birth. What happened?"

"I want a homebirth eventually, but I thought I should have the first at a hospital just to be safe. I was in labor for 32 hours. Fifteen hours after my water broke, they finally did a c-section. The epidural wore off in the middle of the surgery. I could feel everything, so they gave me a mask with general anesthesia. Then they took my baby for 12 hours. I didn't see her for that whole time. They fed her bottles and formula. This is not what I planned. I couldn't feed her from my breast for almost 24 hours. Now breastfeeding hurts, and she is so confused. That's why I'm here. I also probably lost my chance to ever have a vaginal birth."

Gently my curiosity probed, "Mary and I like to educate new moms on how to prepare for childbirth. I would like to see more women have a doula. Is there something that we can explain better that might have helped you decide to hire a doula?"

"Well, to be quite honest, we called a few doulas. Price ranged from a few hundred dollars and up. We just couldn't afford it."

Still trying to validate her concerns I said, "Cesareans work for the physicians. They end the waiting, and the baby gets out. They also pay better. A c-section doesn't work so well for the mother. Looking back over it all now; a long labor, the cesarean, a 12-hour separation, formula use and breastfeeding problems, wouldn't it be worth the money if you could avoid all that next time?"

Like several other new moms I've talked to, this mom had not understood how traumatic birth can be. She was not prepared for the feelings of loss that she experienced in its aftermath. By letting her vent and giving her some information, I hope to help her be better prepared for the next birth.

~♥~

The two largest professional certifying organizations of doulas in North America are Doulas of North America (DONA http://www.dona.org) and Childbirth and Postpartum Professional Association (CAPPA http://www.cappa.net). Both of these organizations maintain online directories of certified doulas by geographic area.

Experienced doula's rates vary per birth depending on experience, geographic area, demand, patient needs, travel time and sliding scale. Without knowing the "doula climate" in one's area, there is no reason to assume that patients cannot afford the labor support.

In fact, a doula must complete three "certification births" in order to become certified as a professional doula. A student doula seeking certification works at these births without expecting monetary payment. Find out through DONA and CAPPA who is pursuing certification in the area. There also is a program called Operation Special Delivery that supports the United States military by providing free doula services during wartime to women who are preparing for and giving birth while their partners are on military deployment.

I stress the importance of using a certified doula, or one pursing certification, because anyone can call herself a doula. On the other hand, the fact that we refer to a doula as a laywoman should not confuse us into thinking that she "lacks credentials." Birth experience, physician references and formal training are all required before someone becomes certified as a doula.

A TWIN HOMEBIRTH

This was Sharon's sixth pregnancy and second homebirth. It would also be her fourth vaginal birth after cesarean (VBAC). All of her babies had been breastfed for at least a year. This time she would be giving birth to two.

Sharon had a healthy, realistic and informed attitude toward this twin birth. I've known her for several years through her doula work and a previous homebirth we both attended. Her optimism rubs off on me. I feel privileged to re-connect with her during her pregnancy.

Photo by Dawn Bond

We hardly ever hear of full-term twins. Sometimes I wonder whether we verbally induce premature twin births by constantly telling women that twins come early? You hear over and over that twins don't go full-term. I am amazed that anyone carrying twins can mentally overcome the power of prophecy by this well-intended warning. I had pointed this observation out to Sharon early in her pregnancy and encouraged her to get mentally fit. Plan to go full term.

At thirty-eight weeks this pregnancy was going well. Both twins were vertex. As in her other pregnancies, Sharon's waters broke spontaneously. I attended her birth in a non-clinical role, camera in hand. I served as photographer for the family but also as a medically-educated support person for the midwives.

I put my camera aside at least once during her labor to give Sharon physical support. Even though I love shooting photos and do not want to miss getting one precious moment on film, I couldn't imagine being at this birth distanced behind a camera (or emotionally removed by scrubs, mask and a sterile field). Providing supportive comfort and reassurance came naturally.

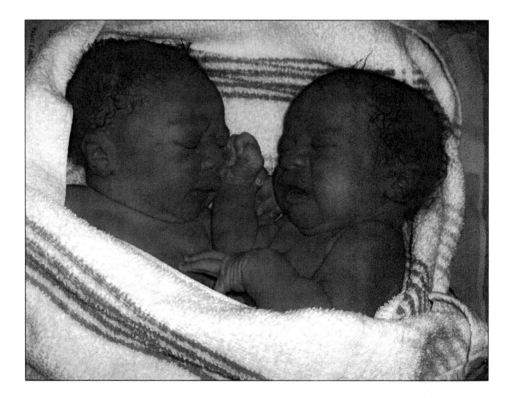

All the attendants and siblings seemed to know their roles, and no one got in each other's way. Dad provided labor support along with the doulas and then caught his babies with guidance from the midwives.

I was curious to see twins nurse right after birth. Would the first twin nurse before the second was born? Would they nurse together? Or one at a time? If so, which one would nurse first? As it turned out, Sharon was having some powerful afterbirth contractions and was not ready to bring them to her breast. The babies were being loved, passed around and photographed. I thoroughly enjoyed preserving these one-of-a-kind memories.

As we lay the newborns together in a towel to take more photos, I thought of Anne Geddes, who photographs images like this. But her images are staged and planned ahead of time in her studio. This was natural and spontaneous.

One of the midwives pointed out that this immediate twin bonding would never have happened if the birth had occurred in a hospital. In a hospital each baby would have had different receiving pediatric teams and separate warmers and routines to undergo.

The two little brothers were skin-to-skin, naked, bonding, cooing and exploring each other. Just what twins should be allowed to do immediately after birth! I had finally made it to another mom's homebirth for the actual birth. I am filled with gratitude for this opportunity to behold this beautiful twin homebirth.

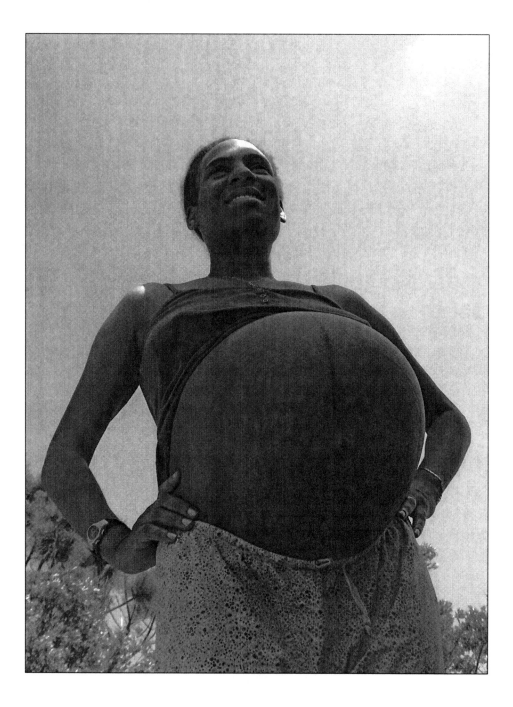

PERMISSION TO BIRTH

The birth center had been closed down for some time. The local hospitals have since banned vaginal birth after cesarean. The circumstances make it hard for the homebirth midwives to continue to offer VBACs. Women are running out of choices for birth. Now it's not unusual for women to consult with me prior to conception or prenatally to find out *what* resources are available for their particular circumstances. The trend of decreased options in birth is not just local, but national. When a woman is willing to drive two hours or more, I can refer her to a birth provider who hasn't caved in to the trend yet. As for the services I myself can provide to birthing women, I offer prescriptions for initial prenatal labs, episodic care during pregnancy, and examination of the newborn.

I met Tina earlier in her pregnancy at an ICAN meeting. Her first birth had been a cesarean. At that time, women were still told they could have future vaginal births. She since had two hospital vaginal births.

Tina formally consulted with me at 38 weeks with her fourth pregnancy after all potential birth providers confirmed they would not deliver her fourth baby by VBAC. Tina's foremost concern was to know if I would be available to examine her baby after her planned unassisted birth. I reassured her I would be.

Tina also had several important questions about the rest of her pregnancy. Birthing unassisted did not mean she ignored her concerns. She wanted to know the options for treating Group B Strep. Together we researched both pharmaceutical and homeopathic options to treat GBS outside the hospital. This was another learning experience for me. There are many ways midwives around the world treat GBS! After all, many of these midwives do not have access to hospitals and IV antibiotics. Tina decided which approach was right for her.

She also wanted to know what options she had if she tore and required stitches. This was a great opportunity to discuss with her laceration prevention. I told her how being in an intuitive position to deliver would make tearing less likely. I also explained that her "outside" tissues would need time to relax and stretch just like the cervix needs time to open. Without medication speeding things up, her birth canal would have time to accommodate. In case she did tear, I also informed her about midwives I had read about when I was pregnant who deliver without access to suture supplies. Their style of being hands off rarely leads to lacerations.

In *Motherwit,* one midwife gave an example of a woman who she did send to the hospital to be sutured for a fourth-degree tear. This mother refused local anesthetic for religious reasons and was sent home without stitches. By strict adherence to bed rest with knees cross, this tear healed. The midwife describes how this woman had an easy second delivery over intact perineum without trace of scar tissue.

I reassured Tina that I felt she could birth naturally. How she went about it (where, with whom…) would be her own decision. I thought I was a uniquely prepared physician to provide office consultation to an unassisted birth because I had been part of several "beginnings and ends" of homebirths.

Tina came in a few hours after her birth at home. Despite a previous cesarean, a positive group B strep, and no medical assistance at birth, her baby was well and nursing well. The shoestring that tied the baby's umbilical cord caught me off guard. I was so used to seeing "a cord clamp" on newborns.

Tina was sore on the bottom and wanted me to check her for tears. Rather than lithotomy position (on her back) and stirrups, I asked her to side lie on my exam table with her hip and knees bent. She could be properly draped. There was no active bleeding and no reason to do an internal exam. I could show her partner where a few small tears were. He could know what to look for if there were more concerns at home. But, by taking it easy the next few days and weeks they should heal without further intervention. I have suturing supplies in the office. I was glad there wasn't a need to use them.

I saw the baby again a few days later for a heel stick test (PKU). Tina informed me that she'd had no problem obtaining a birth certificate. I asked her to call me if she had any concerns about herself or the baby.

~♥~

Deep down, I got the impression that Tina would have preferred to have support with her all the way. She (and many of the other women I have shared about) make birth look easy, and they do seem lucky. This is a good time to re-emphasize that all of these women were very well prepared. They understand what they want out of birth.

I also want to stress that a doula and a midwife are not the same thing. I hear from couples "Well, I have a *midwife*. Why do I need a doula?" They don't realize a midwife has clinical responsibilities (medical information and opinions, diagnosis, prescription, and catching the baby), while a doula is there to help a woman cope physically, emotionally, mentally, and socially with the demands of labor without fear of malpractice and legal constraints.

For example, although she provided massage and reassurance when my labor was still early and uneventful, my midwife needed to focus on the unexpected breech when it happened. She couldn't be my "support" person then. In those same critical minutes, the doulas were there for me. They helped me stay focused and David delivered safely.

This was similar to how I felt as Jayne's physician; I couldn't be protecting Jayne's perineum *and* be at the head of the bed comforting her. I was relieved to have Jayne's doula with us. She made my work go smoother.

DOCTOR, MOTHER AND POLITICAL ADVOCATE

O nce again, I found out that *an obstetrician* had a problem with *my* delivery. More than a year after David's birth, the state's Quality Assurance Division initiated an investigation of my midwife. They received a complaint from an obstetrician I call Dr. Deity. I understand that his concern is about the midwife's scope-of-practice and not about "me" per se. However, as a concerned mother I took the opportunity to present my perspective. We all must take responsibility for our births. The following is my reply (which is slightly edited for context and privacy) to a letter my midwife received from the state addressing his concerns.

Florida Department of Health
Division of Medical Quality Assurance-Investigative Services Unit
1720 East Tiffany Drive, Suite, 202-A
West Palm Beach, Fl, 33407

Dear (Medical Quality Assurance Investigator):
Re: DOH Complaint #MW 2204-19000001

As you know, I have a healthy and thriving 20-month-old son born at a planned homebirth. His footling breech presentation was a surprise to me. Several pairs of professional hands examined my abdomen towards the end of my pregnancy and not one person diagnosed that my son was in the breech position.

I take full responsibility for declining vaginal exams during labor. I am fully confident that I can trust my body and its rhythm during the birth process and did not find it necessary to subject myself to risks of infection, rupture of membranes, and the anti-intuitive position of lying on my back. I was open to vaginal exams or transferring to the hospital if the need arose, but I was comfortable and fetal heart tones were being monitored by dopler and they were stable. In fact, the birth of my second son occurred at the hospital without vaginal exam during labor or electronic fetal monitoring.

I received prenatal care by midwives from the mountains. This birth team was planning to come to my house to deliver my son. I chose not to call them when the time came. I found my midwife was able to meet my needs. I called the midwife from the mountains, the morning after delivery to let them know I delivered. She was surprised that I did not call her to attend the birth; she was fully expecting me to. I led my new midwife to believe that I would call the other midwives also.

I stress, my son is healthy now, and was healthy at the time of birth. I reinforce that this was not a planned footling breech delivery. It seems very silly to penalize my midwife for this 1 ½ years later. I am very satisfied with my birth and outcome. She handled my surprise presentation quite well. There is no health or developmental consequences to either me or my son. My family has happily adjusted to our new family member.

I have since keenly reviewed breech literature and research. I'd like to think that my surprise breech birth was one of a kind and something for me to uniquely brag about. But it is not. Throughout the international midwifery literature I find case reports of planned and unplanned breeches being delivered at home. Unfortunately, in our state and country, women are penalized with cesarean surgery for breech presentation. As such, I have corresponded with two women who have also had undiagnosed breech births at presentation. One was in a hospital and went on to have an immediate cesarean by hospital protocol with major complications and had another immediate subsequent surgery. The other was diagnosed at home, transferred to a hospital, had a cesarean per protocol. It breaks my heart that these mothers went through unnecessary surgery based on presenting part without documentation of fetal distress. Just as general surgeons are efficient now at performing laparoscopic cholecystectomy (gallbladder surgery) and are losing their skills at doing open choly's in an emergency; the art of vaginal delivery is lost. Why can't an obstetrician deliver a (undiagnosed) vaginal breech? Because they are more comfortable managing cesarean!

Sadly enough, the standard-of-care legally protects only the provider (the physician or hospital) and is not necessarily in the best emotional, physical, or spiritual interest of the consumer (the patient).

I feel honored to have the midwife attend my birth and to show my deep appreciation I wrote the articles and decided to put them on the web. Additionally my birth stories have been published in premier midwifery publications—as an educational tool and an example for other midwives!

Also, Dr. Deity complains that my midwife advertises that she "Will travel for footling breech." This statement was a quip accompanying a photo of her and my six-year-old son. It is a caption I made up. It was on my family website, not my midwife's website. I removed it when I got wind of the fact that the obstetrician was investigating this to protect my midwife. Does he really think I let my six-year-old son travel and deliver breech babies? As a mother, I have the right to put what I want on my family website.

I have practiced Urgent Care and Family Medicine with my husband and I have been active in the Treasure Coast mothering community for ten years, even doing volunteer work on the maternity unit where Dr. Deity delivers. Perhaps my colleague should have come to me first if my birth upset him so much. I am easily approachable professionally, and through volunteer organizations serving childbearing women, and I am also easily accessible through e-mail.

To conclude I don't see grounds for an investigation based on my birth experience.

Yours very truly,

Denise Punger MD FAAFP IBCLC

~♥~

The state has no idea how much I prepared for my birth, nor does Dr. Deity. These are the kind of people controlling my births and yours. I never heard anything else from the state after my reply, though I know it was received because I sent it by certified mail.

This government interference with midwifery practice and my birth hit home. It reminds me of government interference in ancient times:

[15]*The king of Egypt spoke to the Hebrew midwives, one of whom was named Shiphrah and the other Puah,* [16] *saying, "When you deliver the Hebrew women, look at the birthstool: if it is a boy, kill him; if it is a girl, let her live."* [17] *The midwives, fearing G-d, did not do as the king of Egypt had told them; they let the boys live.* [18] *So the king of Egypt summoned the midwives and said to them, "Why have you done this thing, letting the boys live?"* [19] *The midwives said to Pharaoh, "Because the Hebrew women are not like the Egyptian women: they are vigorous. Before the midwife can come to them, they have given birth."* [20] *And G-d dealt well with the midwives; and the people multiplied and increased greatly.* [21] *And because the midwives feared G-d, He established households for them.* [22]

---JPS Tanakh 1985

According to rabbinic teachings, Shiphrah and Puah were code names that Moses' mother Jochebed and sister Miriam used in disguising themselves from Pharaoh. "Households" did not mean buildings. Because of their devotion to the Jewish people, they were rewarded with grand dynasties. Jochebed/Shiphrah becomes the ancestress of the Kohanim (the "priests") and the Levites; Miriam/Puah becomes an ancestress of David. How noble was their calling. How appropriate that Moses *was* born to royalty.

But what does this analogy have to do with the current birthing culture? First, all women are like the Hebrew women and can give birth without human (Pharaoh's) interference. The midwives Shiphrah and Puah used non-violent resistance to preserve life. Here, in my rebuttal to the investigation, I am emulating their efforts to protect my birthing rights, as well as the rights of those who come after me. In order to preserve life, I often need to have enough trust and faith to go beyond the standard-of-care of so-called "modern-day" law and medicine.

Women seeking vaginal births after cesarean or other "politically incorrect" births carry on the spirit of these ancient midwives. In preserving life, my identity has been merged with these righteous women. Spiritually speaking I have become a "Midwife."

Finally, don't forget that Moses was born at home. He was breastfed, too.

By this time I could clearly understand why my doulas want to restore Godly confidence to woman to birth their own babies. The medical model of fear-based birth influenced by politics, legal and corporate greed *does not work* for women. Women must be responsible to pursue truth and meaning in childbirth.

I am aware that the Creator of Life rewarded me with a lesson more spiritually powerful than I ever imagined. This has left me as an informed and devoted messenger of the way birth was designed to be.

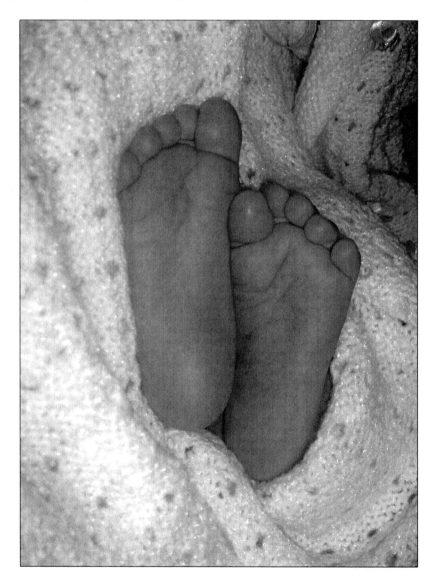

PART 2 – THE BREASTFEEDING YEARS

As my son turned four years old, I was concerned that he was accumulating too many material gifts. I wanted him to enjoy what he was given, but I also wanted to teach him what was most important. After turning the lights out one evening, I asked him, "William, do you know what the most important gift of all is?"
Without a hesitation he stunned me, "Love," he said. I was very proud of him as we cuddled. He thought about my question a little more and then said, "Mom, breastfeeding is love," and he nursed to sleep.

"You're stupid."
"No, you are stupid."
"YOU ARE STUPID."
"You're TWICE as stupid."
"YOU'RE THREE TIMES AS STUPID."
"YOU'RE TEN TIMES AS STUPID."
"YOU'RE HUNDRED TIMES AS STUPID."
"YOU'RE STUPID ALL THE WAY TO INFINITY."
"YOU'RE STUPID ALL THE WAY TO INFINITY AND BEYOND."
"YOU'RE STUPID ALL THE WAY TO INFINITY AND BEYOND, AND BACK."
"Mama's milk made me smart."
"No. It made me smarter."
"Mama's milk made me TWICE as smart..."

"Mom, I wish I had two heads so they could both nurse and I could feel extra good."
"Scott, sometimes I wish you had two heads so you would be done faster."

91

Breastfeeding Didn't Come Natural

Where do I begin to tell the story of how I've nursed three kids over a seven years span, the middle one tandem nursing with both the oldest and then the youngest? Currently, my 7-month-old is exclusively breastfeeding and my 5-year-old will nurse to sleep and upon awakening. He says it's cloud nine. There is no end in sight to his nursing.

I don't want to frighten a new mom away with my extreme breastfeeding example, but I want to be honest about what has worked well for me. A young mom needs to know why I nurse so long, how I felt about it in the beginning, and how I came around. I want to set an example for others so they don't wean due to peer pressure and cultural misinformation before mom and baby are really ready.

My extended nursing didn't happen naturally. Nor did I plan to breastfeed my boys "forever." In fact, I wasn't that dedicated to breastfeeding while I was expecting William. It appeased my peers to say, "Sure, I'll breastfeed."

In my heart, I was going back to work full-time. I was going to be busy. I didn't think I'd have time for pumping and storing. I didn't even know if it made a real difference to breastfed. I had the typical understanding of breastfeeding of any physician/mom right out of residency in 1995. I could have easily been a lactation failure.

William was born a year after my husband and I completed our residencies. John recalled one lecture on infant nutrition during his internship. That was one hour devoted to breastfeeding and infant nutrition in all his eight years of training.

That beat me. I had a lecture, too, but it was about managing infant formula. It is typical of medical schools and postgraduate trainings not to offer much on breastfeeding. After all, the formula manufacturers sponsor the continuing education of doctors and faculty members.

My husband recalled learning that breastfeeding may lead to higher IQs. That was the only benefit to breastfeeding we knew, but this got me thinking that the effort to breastfeed might be worth it.

Before I knew it, I had newborn William at my breast within 30 minutes of his being born. He nuzzled a little. It was a strange feeling to have this new life attached to my nipple. After an exhausting labor—not the labor I had hoped for—we both slept a few hours. The nurse woke me up a few hours later, "He's hungry! Time to nurse." I felt like I had been beaten up and she wanted me to nurse him? This time it hurt. "He's a champ," the nurse ignored my concern. And the next time it hurt, too.

Looking for pity, I complained to the next shift nurse. She said, "Well, it's not for everyone." Her reverse psychology immediately took hold. Don't tell ME, I can't do this. Breastfeeding was going to be for me! Those first two weeks, I had some more unexplained pain with latch. I still doubted that any good could come out of this.

My sister was nursing my 7-month-old nephew. In fact, he was exclusively breastfed. I had a good example. I had to live up to my younger sister's role model. I was glad she did something before me. I recall watching Zachary nurse as he did "aerobics," kicking his leg up and down. I had never seen an "older" baby nurse before—just a few newborns. My nephew's motor activity was weird to me. Wasn't it time to wean if they could move and wriggle while nursing? Yes, I really thought that! My sister gave me good advice for the first weeks. "Make breastfeeding a priority," she said, "To get breastfeeding off to a good start, William needs your patience. He is learning, too." The other thing she recommended was that for the next six months not to make too many outside commitments in advance. Take it one day at a time until I was used to life with a baby.

I had people tell me that I would not like mothering. They thought it was better for me to have a paying career and that my baby would be better off in daycare. Those were some awful things to say because I *was* influenced. People's suggestions have powerful effects, especially when they are wrong.

In those early days, though, contrary to what I was set up to believe about mothering, I had a precious time with my *primogenito*, my first born. (My in-laws' Spanish terms of endearment mean a lot to me.) I listened to my heart. I found that I wanted to do what was best for him, even if it didn't seem to come easy. I wanted him close. I wanted to feel that he was mine. I wanted him to trust me. He was so vulnerable and totally dependent. I wanted to really appreciate all my time with Baby William, especially before going back to work. So many mixed messages for me to process as a new mom.

In preparation for going back to work at three months, I read everything I could get my hands on about pumping breastmilk. I even read formula company brochures—of all places—about how to wean before going back to work at three months. Of course, they're experts on weaning. They want us to buy their products!

Fortunately, I had good instincts. I distinctly recall reading in a going-back-to-work pamphlet written by a formula company, "When your baby is six-weeks-old it is time to introduce one bottle a day the first week, 2-3 bottles the second week, etc…"

Six weeks came fast. I did not want to give my baby a bottle of formula! I was just getting used to this nursing thing. William just melted in my arms every time he latched. It was comforting to me as a mother to see my *precioso* so comfortable at the breast. It was too soon to stop. How could I deny him? At the same time, I was slowly becoming convinced that I wanted to breastfeed for a year. The American Academy of Pediatrics recommended a one-year minimum, and then as long as mutually desired. Could I actually do this for twelve months? One month was already gone. I had 11 more to go.

NURSING IN PUBLIC

Another barrier to overcome was that I was not comfortable breastfeeding in public. I tried various ways. At first, we sought out the lounge area of bathrooms, but most were too dirty, so we looked for dressing rooms. But the thing was, William was a lingering-type nursling. I didn't want to stay cooped up in private for the next year whenever I went out. I tried bringing bottles of my pumped milk. What an inconvenience in South Florida trying to keep milk cool!

But something else inspired me to get over this modesty. When I gave William a bottle of milk myself, it felt so impersonal. I felt like I was betraying him even though he took it willingly. It wasn't the same. I sat near other mothers mixing formula. I felt sorry for them and their babies. It made me long to breastfeed and to feel the closeness.

After experimenting with various ways of feeding a baby in public, I finally became resigned to letting William drink directly from me in public. No bottles, no coolers. I got used to a wardrobe of two-piece outfits and nursing tops and bras that are nursing-friendly. I eventually found out that wearing your baby in a sling is a great way to nurse and have privacy. I found myself wanting to set a good example of infant feeding. I *became* embarrassed to have the bottles. I am not a breastfeeding mother who wants to nurse right in your face. However, I do like to dress discreetly and I don't mind that strangers know *how* I am feeding my baby.

NURSING AFTER CONCEPTION

Before long I was approaching the one-year mark in nursing William. Friends, family and co-workers said, "He is getting ready to wean." This didn't make sense, nor did it ring true to what I was experiencing. By the time William was 13 months old I was pregnant again, and he certainly didn't seem to be weaning.

"Oh, he will," I heard.

"The milk will go sour,"

"It will turn to colostrum."

Still, William didn't wean himself.

"You *have* to wean him before the baby," Someone insisted. "How could you feed two?"

And the most confusing response, "Don't let him do that to you."

Do what to me? Let me know I was the center of his little universe? Need me for the nourishment that my body is designed to give him? This was "doing something to me?" Actually, nursing was the only time my active toddler sat still. It was the only time I could rest and close my eyes. Often, we would fall asleep together to get some much-needed refreshing sleep. I didn't want to wean him.

Before I had my own children, I once heard of tandem nursing–nursing all the way through a subsequent pregnancy and then breastfeeding the two siblings together. This hearsay turned out to be a prophetic in my case.

TANDEM NURSING, ONE DAY AT A TIME

I had heard tandem-nursing moms say that when their newborn milk came in the older child reveled in the fresh milk and both siblings would nurse non-stop. I heard these moms talk about feeling "touched out," like they were exhausted with being touched. But at about two months postpartum, they said, the honeymoon would be over for the older kid, and they would wean themselves.

I gave birth to Scott and began tandem nursing. Two months went by, then three, four, five and six months. These boys still nursed all the time! I was extremely touched out. Yet, I had times that I really looked forward to nursing, for example, when I walked in the door after working all day. Even though I pumped at work, the "milk jugs" were full. When both of my sons nursed, it was a reunion. It felt good to see their contentment. After the flow slowed down, their suck pattern would change, and I went back to feeling "annoyed" as they

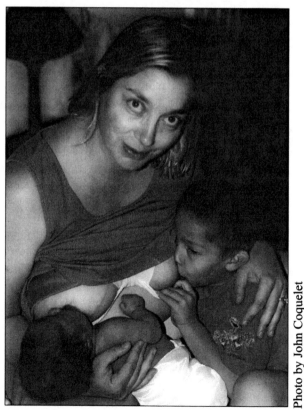

Photo by John Coquelet

101

continued to suckle most of the evening.

These two boys nursed all night. We slept in a family bed, one boy on each side of me. I nursed one, and then I rolled over and nursed the other. Before one was done the other would be crying again for a turn. It was exhausting. I felt like a freak.

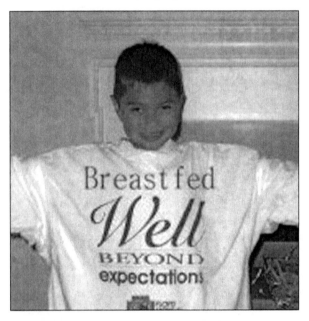

This was about the time I started seeking breastfeeding support. I wasn't sure if I wanted reassurance, information, inspiration or weaning techniques. In any case, some days it seemed like none of it helped. Other days it seemed like bits and pieces were helpful.

Going over a list of all the reasons why breastfeeding is so important helped me get through one day at a time. That's why I was so receptive when I was approached to give advice on the manuscript of a then upcoming new book, *Breastfeeding: Your Priceless Gift to Your Baby and Yourself,* which presents twenty to-the-point benefits summarizing the emotional and physical benefits of breastfeeding for the mother, baby, family, and society. Once again, I could get the reassurance I needed through involving myself in the intimate process of editing.

The other thing that gave me continuous inspiration during that time was to inspire other moms to breastfeed. I became committed to the community through the Breastfeeding Task Force. I also became committed to passing the IBCLC exam. As a physician with my interests, it wouldn't be too difficult to meet the requirements to sit for the exam. I studied. I attended conferences. I passed. Becoming a breastfeeding mother had made quite an impact on my life!

ON WEIGHT GAIN

I was surprised at how many people think tandem nursing would lead to malnourishment and prematurity. My boys were all nine pounds at birth. I gained 50 pounds during each of the first two pregnancies. My son William was 23 months old when Scott delivered at 41 weeks. William nursed three to five times each day towards the end of my pregnancy. William nursed himself to sleep the night I went into labor with Scott. I actually enjoyed the times I was able to sit still with him.

By four months old, William was already to 20 pounds. Scott, too, doubled his weight by the time he was four months.

William gained weight quickly after Scott was born. He went from about 30 to 40 pounds in three months. It must have been all that rich early breastmilk. His soiled diapers looked like an exclusively breastfed infants: filled with yellow seedy looking stool. Obviously they were not deprived of any nutrition. My appetite remained healthy.

I didn't pay attention to who nursed first or which side. Basically, they were both content on the breast and both cried when off. I didn't want to hear the crying, so they both nursed.

Both of my boys continued to nurse together three to five times or more daily. I have done a lot of research on tandem nursing, but there is not much written on what happens beyond three or four months. From my own research and personal experience, I don't see why a mother should routinely be told not to tandem nurse or nurse through a pregnancy. I confidently nursed through my third pregnancy.

A CASE FOR THE FAMILY BED

It's getting really crowded in my bed, but I would not insist on changing our nighttime co-sleeping routine until the boys are ready. I love seeing them when they are sleeping. They look angelic. Reading together and falling asleep together is a loving routine. For me it is easier than other kinds of bedtime schedules. Waking up together is even more enjoyable. The mood is special in the morning. When we have a chance to linger in bed, it is my favorite time of sharing and intimacy with the boys.

On days that we are busy as adults, bed-sharing makes up for lost time. Sleeping together is also healing for them as they go through emotionally difficult times. I remember when I was single, studying, and not dating, nighttime was a lonely time, and that's when I was an adult! I would not expect or want my young ones to be separated at night and have to tolerate unwanted alone time. Besides, they can't be in trouble if they are next to me, nor is there any reason to be "scared of the dark."

Bed-sharing means fewer sheets to wash and fewer beds to make. Sometimes a child will wake up at night and ask me to take him to the bathroom. I suspect that if he woke up alone, he might not go to the toilet and wet the bed instead, and then I would incorrectly diagnose that as enuresis.

Bed-sharing is environmentally friendly in other ways, too. If you want, you can regulate the temperature in just one room. It saves on heat because the extra bodies generate heat. And when we travel, we take up only one room.

Finally, of course, bed-sharing makes breastfeeding at night a lot easier. When you nurse side-lying and you learn how to sleep through the feeding, breastfeeding becomes a part of your night instead of it taking over.

MORE ABOUT OUR FAMILY BED

My kids love sleeping with me. In the beginning, I thought co-sleeping with a baby was unacceptable.

I found myself exhausted during the first days at home. It turned out that napping with William was surprisingly refreshing. I looked forward to these naps. William could nurse while I kept my eyes closed and rested. I couldn't see how harm could come from taking a nap together. Yet, I doubted myself. It seemed so against everything I was ever told. There were isolated times (and with guilt) I brought William into the bed at night. These arrangements worked. Yet, it would be awhile before I was at peace (free of what others might say) with him in our bed all the time.

By the time Scott was born, I had read Dr. Sears' *The Baby Book* and another book *The Family Bed.* I was now confident that bed-sharing was in my children's best interest. We'd have no loss time. Scott even slept in the hospital bed with me. At home, occasionally, newborn Scott and I went to another room with a bathroom closer to the bed for my sake. The bed was easier for me to get in and out of, too. Scott never went in the crib that was set up in our master bedroom. We got rid of it once we knew that Scott liked sleeping with us. Believe it or not, I never set up a room to be a "nursery" or used a "monitor" for any of the boys. The first house was too small, and after that it wasn't important to our arrangement.

I liked napping with Scott, too. Since William always wanted to nurse at the same time, often we all fell asleep together. I nicknamed our sleep-time as "tandem-nursing naps." I found these naps to be some of the best sleep I ever got (or maybe I just was more exhausted). I could have lain there forever snuggling with my two amazing sons.

David was brought right into bed with the four of us. For a short time we all five slept as straight as logs in the big bed. When we moved to the house we still live in now, we left the bed frame behind. I have a new full mattress lying on the floor next to the king mattress in our master bedroom. We have plenty of room for all of us to sleep. However, with parents' sharing office hours and call coverage, we don't all occupy the bed at the same time.

The boys love for me to read to them when they fall asleep. That's the time when I read the fairy tales and other stories they love to hear over and over. I've thought about moving them to another bed, but I've never figured out how to duplicate our reading time with everyone separated. Many times reading relaxes me, and I can go to sleep without getting up, again. Prior to settling, the boys love jumping on the mattresses and singing, "No Jumping on Mama's Bed," playing peek-a-boo, and hiding in a "tent." One thing I have been able to be consistent about is being there at night for the boys. They can decide when they want their own beds.

TUB TIME

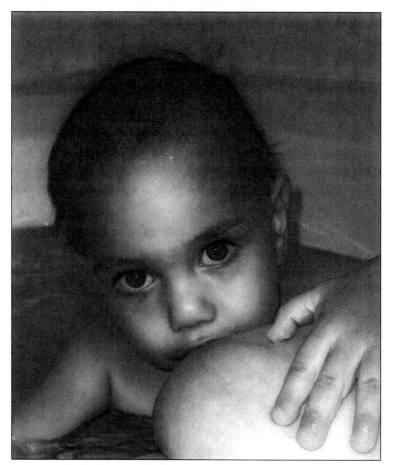

Every time we moved, I have always been fortunate to have an oversized bathtub. I received conflicting information about when we could begin going in the tub. I found what worked for me: co-bathing starting with the first week. There was no lost time co-bathing with any of the boys. I didn't fill the tub when I brought in my infants. I'd use just enough water to soothe my bottom. I could put my newborn across my chest to nurse or have him lying in a vertical position with his back supported on my flexed legs facing me. Just because his umbilicus couldn't be immersed didn't mean that I couldn't position him creatively or that I couldn't lather him elsewhere. I especially enjoyed lathering my sons' hair, because I loved the soft downy look of their freshly clean newborn hair. Nursing a baby in a tub is very comforting and relaxing.

Now, I don't believe babies routinely need a bath within hours of birth. That's a hospital policy. The vernix, the newborn coating, protects the baby from its new environment and should not be washed off immediately. Unfortunately, we are culturally trained to believe newborns are dirty. My first two babies got their routine hospital baths. My intent with David was to hold off a few days. However, he stooled on his way out and ended up being covered in meconium. He needed some spot cleaning with lavender and water. He got his "bath" in my presence on our family bed.

A bath is stimulating for a baby's sensory development. Skin-to-skin contact, water texture, bubbles, massage, and scents are all beneficial.

Exclusively breastfed babies poop with nearly every feed the first six weeks after the first week. It must feel really good to them to soak in a bath after diaper blowouts. Parents may also bring a baby into the shower. Babies can bathe or shower with either parent. Just hold on tight to them. It's popular to bathe baby in a sink. We did some of that, too. I also gave sponge baths and massages to my babies.

As the boys became more mobile, the tub was the place we could go together to relax where I didn't have to chase a toddler. All of mine were happy to stay in it and play and nurse. They all liked to nurse wrapped in their towel after the bath.

Throughout the day I am on the go and distracted. The bath brings me back to baby. Tub time is good quality time together. Like everything else in mothering, they'll be someone to say, "He's too young to take in the bath." And then you'll soon hear, "He is too old." So how long should you share a bath? For our family, the boys decide.

SLING MUSINGS

Baby experts often claim that babies must get used to soothing themselves right from the start. When I was pregnant with my first baby, we acquired every baby care item under the sun to "comfort" a little one. I had and did not need a playpen for the living room, a cradle in the master bedroom and a crib over-crowding another room. I did not need a bouncy seat, a big round jumping saucer, AND a swing: Just one of these would have been sufficient. We had a mobile, *two* hanging play gyms, and toys with black and white patterns that were supposed to improve eye development, even though William had what I would eventually learn is the most important visual—my face!—to gaze at while he was breastfeeding. We offered a rubber pacifier, but as thriving breastfed babies usually do, he rejected it. The first time around mothering I thought my baby would miss some important developmental goal if I didn't have it all.

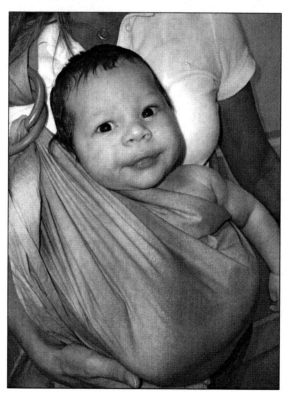

Five years later, I had gotten rid of all the baby items. When they heard the news of my third pregnancy, well-intended people often said, "It's a shame you don't have any of your stuff anymore." Without hesitation I'd reply, "Please don't replace it!" By then, I knew that modern babies still prefer their mother's breasts and cuddling.

Co-sleeping, co-bathing, and babywearing, are components of skin-to-skin care. They are the true methods that babies love. These activities benefit each other and influence breastfeeding. Wearing your baby, like co-sleeping and co-bathing, is a technique for your baby to feel nurtured and loved and know its importance in your family's structure. Wearing your baby helps to blend a new baby into your life.

As far as babywearing goes, I didn't start off so confident. With my first baby, William, I had a structured front carrier from a department store. It was a hand-me-down from my sister who had had a five-pound baby that remained light throughout his in-arms phase.

I, on the other hand, birthed a baby who was always beyond the top of the growth

curve. His ounces turned to tons in this improperly fitting front carrier. (By the way, many commercial carriers don't support the baby's legs properly. Their hips should be flexed, not dangled.) This carrier put all the weight on my shoulders, so I didn't use it for long. I also went through various strollers. I tried compact strollers, luxury strollers and jogging strollers, trying to find the perfect way to take a baby out.

While pregnant the second time, I came across the websites promoting padded ring slings. I wanted to hold and rock my babies. I found it hard to take my eyes off my little ones! So I tried the sling to achieve the closeness I desired.

Right away, I loved the feel and the comfort of having my baby curled up in the sling, his belly to my belly. It made it easy to cradle my baby in my arms as much as I wanted. I could joyfully hear his coos and feel peace in the rhythm of his breathing as I gazed down on him.

I carried him all the time for three months. After that I stopped because of Scott's large size and my resulting backache. I continued to see older babies being carried by mothers and missed not being able to do the same.

After I had my third baby, it was a great joy to have a newborn to tote and comfort in this same sling. I really love that feeling. But David quickly seemed to outgrow it. Once again, ounces turned to tons and my back began to hurt. Being more sling savvy now and appreciating the benefits of closeness, I wanted to find a carrier that would work.

I tried another chain-store type front carrier for a while. When David became a "hip" baby, the carrier didn't feel right anymore. Again, the weight was too much on my shoulders. I happened to find a stretchy mesh fabric that I simply tied in a big loop with a knot and used that as a sling. My homemade sling worked well and eventually helped me to realize that my original padded sling did not have enough fabric. Had it been six to twelve inches longer it would have better accommodated my growing babies (and my own growing hips) and distributed the weight more evenly across my back while the boys grew. I could have used a sling all along if I had a proper fitting one and all the facts.

Since my third birth, my doula started sewing slings. She was available to listen to all the problems with the slings I had tried. She made a non-padded sling for me. I loved it! I happily, continued to use her style sling most of the time. I like the lack of bulk.

My coordination with the sling gets better all the time. After a year or so, my son could support himself enough that I could slide him over onto my back. That set my hands free while I checked out at a cash register or went through a buffet line. I have also found that I could breastfeed in the sling without taking it off. Or perhaps I should say that my squirming toddler had found positions to breastfeed in that worked for him. At age 1 ½, he weighed 26 pounds. I was very comfortable. Since I have carried him continuously since birth one way or another, my body had accommodated to his growth.

I get compliments all the time about the sling. Often, people want to know where to get one. My doula continues to make them! And I teach new moms how to use them! She uses rings that are designed to support the riggings of a sailboat, so they are guaranteed to support far more than the weight of a child. When I think how much I spent trying different strollers in the earlier years, it's a lot more economical to buy that "piece of fabric."

Even better than the economy are the convenience and safety. My son likes being close to me. I don't have to worry about him climbing out of the sling like he might with a stroller or wagon. Many admirers joke that they would hardly recognize me without my hip attachment.

At about 2 ½ years old my son preferred to walk most of the time. Still, if he was extremely tired or sick, or if we had a long walk, he liked to be on my back. I was happy to let him. I carried him as much as I could in my sling. I want to protect my back as I enjoy his sweet baby-love as long as possible. Before long he will outgrow me.

I learned to use the wrap with five yards of material, which is another way to wear your baby. It's trickier and harder to learn, but worth it. The last time I wore him was on a day trip to Savannah when he was almost three. There is lots of walking and climbing on uneven cobblestone and pavement. It's not easy to have a stroller downtown or on the River Walk. It felt so good to have him up high, not dragging behind and calling, "C'mon David, Don't touch that. C'mon, *vamos*" In his simple innocence of youth, I overheard a boy about David's age ask, "Daddy, please carry me like that little, boy." I felt so good knowing I was meeting David's needs.

SWITCHING TO CLOTH

It took three babies before I became open to trying cloth diapers. So why did I have everything before but cloth? A lot of it has to do with the false choices new mothers are offered: Instead of "cloth or disposable," we hear, "Huggies or Pampers?" Then the answers become: the brand on sale; the one I got a coupon for this week; the one that brainwashed me with more advertising than the other. The brand names are so familiar we don't even call them diapers anymore.

Besides, my mother told me how horrible cloth diapers were. "Whenever I left the house with a baby I had to take a big sack for clean diapers and a big sack for dirty ones and lug them both everywhere. Paper diapers are the best things that ever happened for mothers." So I was relieved to have had my babies in modern times and I toilet trained two boys without ever owning even one cloth diaper.

It's true that cloth diapers are bulkier. They don't contain little chemical-laden beads for absorption, but I've considered that a good thing ever since I got the inside scoop from a friend living in Atlanta. Her fiancée couldn't live close to her in the city. He needed to live out in the country near his work at the factory that makes the absorptive stuffing for disposable diapers. The reason that the factory was way out in the country is that if it blew up, it would destroy Atlanta. Interesting, that is the stuff we put on our babies' bottoms for two to four years.

I really didn't expect to like cloth. I thought they were dated. I searched on the Internet to see if a person could still find some of these old-fashioned cotton diapers; perhaps on some obscure website. But when I searched, over a thousand sites came up, many of which were owned by stay-at-home mothers! I had a choice of pre-folds, fitted, diaper liners, nighttime diapers, diaper doublers, flannel, terry cloth, cotton, and organic bamboo. I was overwhelmed at first, but with this many sites and choices I concluded that cloth diapers must not be as outdated as I thought.

What cemented my decision to switch to cloth diapers, though, was the cartoon printed across the front of the disposable diaper. The picture was of a baby lamb drinking out of a bottle. Every third or fourth diaper that I pulled out had that print. I don't remember seeing pictures of bottles on the diapers of my first two boys, but in any case I wasn't interested in dressing my third breastfed baby as an advertisement for formula feeding.

While my first two boys were in diapers I wasn't aware of anyone who used cloth. By the time my third son was born, I actually knew a few cloth diaper moms. "I can, too," I decided. The first cloth diapers I ordered were "all-in-ones." Structurally they are fashioned like disposables; the waterproof liner and absorptive layer are attached, and they close with Velcro tabs. In other words, no pins involved. I ordered six off the Internet without having seen them in person. When they arrived I was surprised by how big they looked compared to the disposables, but I was very impressed with the soft flannel lining that would be against my baby's skin. I put one on him. The dipes looked comfortable and the soft interior, irresistible.

We went through those six diapers really fast. I was hooked on the softness, which convinced me this was worth it. I washed them all right away to keep him in the cloth. Then I ordered twenty more. I couldn't wait to get them because I was doing way too many loads every five diapers. (It made me realize how much waste is put into the environment, and how many trees destroyed, in the making of diapers!) For me, washing a load of diapers turned out to be easier than carrying disposables to the trashcan and buying them weekly. Our trash collectors only came once a week, so the diaper odor used to accumulate. With cloth diapers, that problem was gone.

Switching to cloth was one thing my husband easily agreed with. The initial investment seems like a lot all at once, but in the end you are ahead. No running to the store for diapers. No more spending $30-40 each week for disposables. If I had started in cloth with the first baby, I would have saved even more money since the diapers would have been passed on to the next child.

Ignorance abounds on the subject of diapering. For example, one of my relatives expressed concern that the wetness of cloth would give David a rash. She had the idea that paper diapers were healthier because they "pull wetness away." This is a perfect example of how effective advertising can be at spreading misinformation. The truth is that with proper use and washing, cloth is healthier by being less irritating and chemical-free. Moms actually report rash less with cloth diapers. The chemicals in disposables can actually pull too much healthy moisture off of a baby's skin.

Due to the widespread use of disposables, the art of cloth diapering has been lost. I got in with an online network of cloth diapering moms to exchange ideas, and they've taught me so much. Daytime diapers should be checked every hour and changed at least every two hours, or immediately if soiling occurs. Two hours comes fast. If you are used to disposables you probably don't change and throw a diaper out that fast, even though you're supposed to. You do your errands with the assurance that a diaper will last until you're done, and you won't be bothered with diaper changes while you're out. At least, that's how it was for me. With cloth you do have to estimate how many hours you will be out and prepare accordingly. I don't mind this, though. I feel better knowing that I am giving this extra attention to my son's habits.

It took me a few weeks to get into a changing and laundering routine, and I've had some challenges in staying all-natural. For example, I traveled out-of-town with my baby. But I had the forethought to plan around when I would be near a washing machine. We made it ten days traveling in cloth. Another time I was on crutches for two weeks, and at first I was nervous about it. But it turned out to be much easier to wash the diapers than go downstairs and down our sloped driveway to take bags of garbage out.

People warned me, "When you start work or when he starts eating solids you will tire of the cloth." That only made me more committed. Now I am back at work, and my baby gets to model his dipes so we can show other moms that this is both doable and fashionable.

Speaking of work, I have even discovered medical reasons to recommend cloth diapers. The paper diapers are so good at hiding urine that parents can't tell when their newborn is wet. Putting a cloth diaper on the baby is a better way to get accurate information about urine output. Especially for babies with urine output problems, such as poor milk intake or a congenital kidney problem, it is easier to count wet cloth diapers.

The original treatment for congenital hip dysplasia is double diapering. Cloth diapers are bulky enough to use this way. They can be folded in a way to be "double."

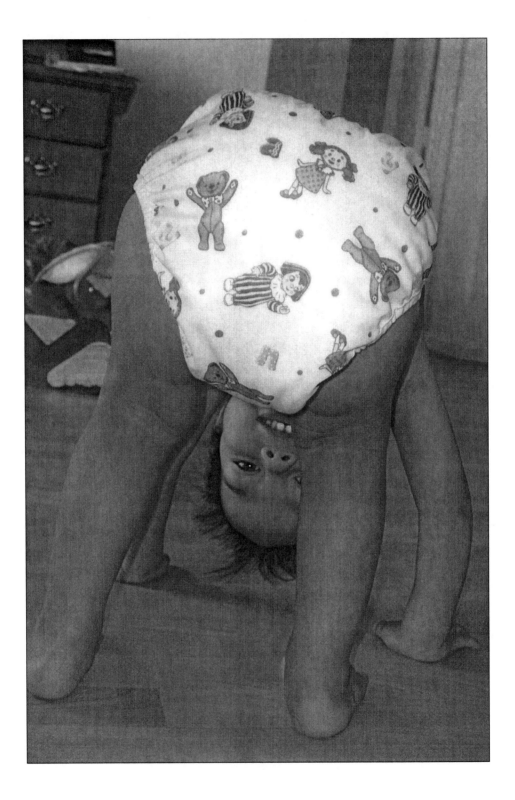

A WORD ABOUT WIPES

Thanks to cloth diapers, I have peace of mind that I'm doing some more good for my baby and the environment: I minimize the use of commercial wipes for the same reason, and I encourage new parents to do the same. If you're at all concerned about the chemicals in diapers, think about what's in wipes. The breastfed baby tends to soil nearly every feed from the first week or so of life through six or eight weeks. Think about it: feces, diapers, chemicals in the wipes, and diaper ointment. That is a lot of repetitive irritation on a newborn's bottom. Naturally the question follows, "What do you use, if you don't use a wipe?"

My recommendation is warm water from the faucet on a cotton baby-sized wash towel, plus a daily bath. Warm water on cloth is so much more soothing than a cold wipe. You may find that your baby doesn't cry during a diaper change anymore. Adult sized washcloths may be to be too thick to get into small crevices, but baby washcloths are just the right size and launder easily. They can also be washed with cloth diapers. Better yet, cotton wipes don't cost much compared to the convenient wipes.

If you're going to be away from home, you can keep a few washcloths with a little water in a sealed bag. In the case of messy blow-outs that would use half of a bag of disposable wipes, cotton wipes are much more efficient and absorbent. This means less irritation to baby, quicker clean-ups, and less garbage. And by the way, a blow-out is a good thing. It's a sign of good milk intake.

If you feel you must have a disposable wipe for traveling or emergencies, then just limiting the wipes to these times is a good start. If switching cold turkey to cloth is overwhelming, just go slowly. Try the diapers first or the wipes first. Just get a few and see how it goes. It's worth the investment. Your baby won't associate diaper changing with harsh skin irritation. Instead, diaper changing can be a time of continued bonding for you and your baby.

A Visit to the Pediatrician

In a bit of a shock I walked into the pediatrician's office with my feverish 3-month-old David and a barking 5-year-old Scott. This was the first time ever that I had found it necessary to bring my breastfed boys in for a sick visit. Looking around the waiting area helped me put the situation into perspective as I immediately realized my boys weren't very ill compared to the other children there. With a glance I saw at least twenty babies that were coughing, flushed, fretful and had swollen faces. They were in various containers (car seats and strollers), being rocked by an adult's foot or extended arm. Within the assortment of propped bottles, I noticed a variety of colored beverages for this sick group of kids. None resembled breastmilk.

I carried David in a sling. He was nursing. Scott and William, somewhat obedient, followed me in. I was acutely aware that my babywearing style of parenting was unique. "How could these babies be well?" I thought. "Does anyone else breastfeed, and why is everyone afraid to hold her baby?"

I had brought the two younger boys in at my husband's insistence. I felt like leaving and telling John that we shouldn't be here at all. But I sat, waiting and breastfeeding, hoping that maybe my ease would positively influence someone else to cradle a fussy baby.

Finally, the nurse called us back. I explained to the doctor that this visit was really about putting John at ease. "David's had a fever since yesterday. But he nursed and peed as I'd expect. He was cranky, but consolable by my rocking him all day. Scott woke up in the middle of the night 'barking like a seal,' but he is otherwise fine. Actually, both boys are better since this morning."

I explained with more detail, "I am home with them all day. John is not with them as much. He doesn't know all their cues as I do. He wanted extra reassurance 'from a pediatrician' because the boys are *never* sick." Everything looked good on both boys as the pediatrician examined them. Their lungs were clear. They didn't need chest x-rays or breathing treatment as John feared. I could tell by looking at the waiting room that this doctor was used to giving antibiotics out of necessity. She closed the visit with diffidence, "I don't think they'll benefit from cough syrup, either, but I feel like I haven't done anything."

"Oh, you've done a lot," I assured her. I was so relieved not to have to deal with the practice of defensive medicine, prescribing "just in case." "You've reassured John! I don't want any antibiotics or any medication. I didn't even want to drag the boys in. In fact, I'll make a deal with you right now. If I have a concern about the boys, I will be less hesitant to bring them in, now that I know my questions will be answered without an overuse of medication." So by the time I left, we were all reassured. My pediatrician did more than she could know. Wouldn't it be nice if we could all feel this safe seeking health care?

SCOTT IN THE MIDDLE

Scott didn't want to give up being little for being in the middle. Expecting another baby is an adjustment that is difficult for any child, but for Scott this also meant sharing his night-nights again! It hadn't been long since his older brother, William, stopped asking to nurse.

William has always been a champion of nursing. His desire to nurse was stronger than mine in the beginning. Going back to work full-time when he was 12-weeks-old and pumping milk for him in my absence didn't stop him. He nursed greedily before I left for work and upon my return. "They" were all his on my days off and at nights. Even near the end of my second pregnancy with only colostrum didn't faze him. He was a busy toddler and I looked forward to the rest I got when he was nursing. William adjusted easy to all situations. My having Scott didn't slow him down, either.

Newborn Scott nursed solo while we were in the hospital. My milk came in quickly. Once we got home, William was right there with Scott *every time*. This was frustrating, but from my reading I was prepared for the feeling of being "touched-out." I could surrender to the demands of mothering two male nurslings.

Other tandem-nursing mothers suggested that the older nursling will get bored and wean, or at least slow down after a few weeks or so. But not William! I craved to nurse Scott alone and savor the delicate newborn latch. William's latch was so strong it could suck up the ocean, so it felt. And I often wondered how Scott as a baby felt always having a sibling attached on the other side.

In Scott's early months, William would hold his little brother's hand or stroke his head. As Scott got older the brothers weren't as loving to each other. They would cry and bother each other, as space became limited on my lap. I attempted to put limits on William, but when William decided it was time to nurse, it *was* time. Treats, toys, playmates did not distract him. And he would throw tantrums if he didn't nurse. It was easier for me to deal with being touched out than hear the crying. I would think Scott could relax at the breast better if William was nursing rather than screaming.

Birthdays passed. I tandem nursed one year, two years, three years, then four record-breaking years. Both boys nursed regularly and every day. After Scott's fourth birthday, William slowed down. He started again after our family relocated. Finally my third pregnancy was timed with a waning of William's nursing. Scott got them all to himself and continued to nurse several times daily. He never indicated if the milk turned yuck. I never had any medical problems nursing while pregnant. I had no contractions and I had good weight gains.

Scott wasn't sure if he wanted a baby in the family. In optimistic anticipation of his brother's birth we told him that babies come with a lot of milk. My milk did come in quickly again, and Scott was happy about that. Like his older brother, Scott would hold his baby brother's hand and pet his head as they shared nursing. Scott was already five by now, and his requests to nurse did slow down. He would look lovingly as David relaxed at the breast and ask, "Is he in La La Land?" Scott showed respect for David's space.

When William was three, Scott nursed beside him. When Scott was three,

William was still there. Now that David is three, I finally get to nurse solo again. But my solo nurser has two hands. He always wants to rub the opposite nipple when he nurses, which is annoying.

"David, stop rubbing. It bothers me."

"But, Mom, it doesn't bother me."

I sometimes wish the other side was occupied by a baby.

SURVIVING ANESTHESIA

All my sons had some type of anesthesia while they were breastfed. My oldest son had urologic surgery when he was seven months old. He had an epidural and light general anesthesia. In anticipation, my husband and I lost more sleep than William. On the scheduled day, I was told not to nurse for four hours prior. Quietly however, I decided that if necessary I would nurse up to two hours prior because my crying baby wouldn't understand NPO (nothing by mouth). He wouldn't understand why I couldn't comfort him. My research showed that clear liquids are permitted up to two hours prior to sedation. I also found where newborns were permitted to nurse up to two hours before sedation.

There was no aspiration or other consequence. I got to carry William to the OR myself. While he was still in my arms, an anesthesia mask was placed on him. He was quickly asleep. I put him on the bed and I left the OR. The procedure was quick, so I had William back in my arms in no time at all. He nursed as soon as he was ready. His recovery went well.

My second son had brief mask anesthesia to release his tongue-tie at six weeks. They put a mask on his mouth and nose, moved it away to do the procedure and replaced the mask just when needed to give him more. He wasn't NPO more than two hours, and after the procedure he nursed as soon as he indicated he was ready.

My third son was also sedated twice with oral medication for dental work. He was less than two years old the first time. He was NPO for two hours and nursed as soon as he was awake.

Formula, on the other hand, requires a six-hour NPO period. It is harder to digest and offers no immunologic protection after a procedure. The hospital policies for NPO in babies are often based on the formula-fed example.

MY SPIRITUAL JOURNEY AS PHYSICIAN, MOTHER AND IBCLC

My doulas and I hashed out our births and attachment parenting experiences often. I continued adding detail to my birth stories as my writing skills improved and my understanding deepened. I eventually added details about the spiritual side of David's birth. My doulas wanted to know why I didn't discuss the spiritual journey I traveled at the time of David's birth. They asked whether I might have been more likely to discuss my spiritual needs if I'd had a Jewish doula. The best reply I could offer is that actions speak louder than words. By being available to me throughout my pregnancy, my doulas *were* meeting my spiritual needs.

Still, my friends are right about the fact that my spirituality takes a different form than theirs. I understand my own religious tradition, Judaism, far more than I used to, and that's largely because I have participated in their spiritual activities. In thanks to all of my friends who generously share their spiritual life with me, I want to share a religious tradition that turned out to hold great spiritual meaning for me.

I put a lot of consideration into whether or not to have a *bris*, which is a ritual circumcision. I needed to search my heart to learn if it was really important to me as a spiritual rite. When Jewish women are pregnant and planning (or struggling with the idea) of a *bris*, it is a Torah-based journey of its own.

Deciding to have a bris was especially difficult for me, because the breastfeeding and attachment parenting circles I travel in are so often anti-circumcision.

When I was expecting our first son, my husband John insisted that the circumcision had to be done. I was hoping that my Peruvian husband would forget. I didn't understand him. Latin families don't usually circumcise their sons. On the other hand, Jewish families usually do want a circ, but here I was the one that didn't want to. I had practiced circumcision as a medical resident, but there was no meaning in that for me. The indecision ended when the pediatrician diagnosed a minor problem. He said that a routine newborn circumcision was contraindicated and he recommended a medically necessary circumcision when he became a little older.

We were referred to a pediatric urologist. He suggested doing the circ with an epidural and light general anesthesia. He said that boys his age (seven months) heal and forget it very quickly. He was right. He was crawling and playing that very night.

The pediatrician in the hospital per protocol circumcised my next son, Scott. My husband wanted the boys to look alike, so that's what decided it that time.

Prior to my third son, I learned that some Christian women were seeking *mohelim*, those who are specially trained to follow Jewish law to perform circumcisions. I never gave much thought to the difference between a *bris* and a circumcision before that, or if I was consciously aware of a difference.

Here is what I was expecting and told about a ritual *bris*. First of all, it is a covenant and a baby naming ceremony. Second, there is health reason for waiting until the eighth day of life: blood-clotting factors have matured, the possibility of newborn jaundice is behind, and bonding has occurred. After a week, moms are often feeling better and can perhaps dote on baby more confidently. Also, and very important, unlike hospital newborn circumcisions that are done in the nursery, away from the parents, often before breastfeeding is established, a *bris* is done after breastfeeding is established. Nursing *can be used* to console the baby.

The circumcision is usually done in a synagogue or at home. The baby also gets to suck on gauze soaked with kosher wine for anesthesia and comfort. I had mixed feelings about the wine. It wasn't about giving "alcohol" to a baby, but being the assertive IBCLC (International Board Certified Lactation Consultant) that I have become; I wanted my baby to be exclusively breastfed for six months without introduction of anything else to alter gut flora.

I turned to an international breastfeeding forum to ask experienced Orthodox Jewish lactation consultants how they felt about this little bit of wine. The few responses I did get from IBCLC's did not think the few drops would be enough to alter flora. The replies came with disclaimers. Some were merely silly ("I am not Jewish, but I have been to a *bris*") while others where cruel and misinformed ("Even though I am responding to your question, I don't believe in genital mutilation"). My soul was feeling a bit wounded. I asked the *mohel* if we could soak the gauze with breastmilk. "No," he said. I got the impression this was a non-negotiable ritual. As grounded in the idea of "nothing but breastmilk" I am, I put the gut flora issue behind me. I liked the idea of anesthesia.

John didn't understand why it was important to me to select a *mohel*. I just kept it simple: we had a homebirth and it went better than expected. Now let's have a circ done at home. It will probably go better, too. The *mohel* happened to be a physician, too, which was important to my husband. The *mohel* was from the nearest synagogue 65 miles away. I'm glad he came to us because I still wanted to enjoy my "babymoon" (time with my newborn) by staying home as long as possible.

The *mohel* started the *bris* by saying, "Babies don't like this, but hopefully they will appreciate it when they are older." I applaud him for acknowledging the pain and giving it meaning. The *mohel* did use a restraint board, and I didn't insist otherwise. He gave David three wine-saturated gauze pads to suck on.

During the procedure the *mohel* gave me a Hebrew transliteration to read. The timing of this reading served to distract me from what was going on, and it worked. I didn't grasp the full meaning of the Hebrew blessing, but I was aware of reading something with enormous meaning. By the time I was done concentrating on the words, the procedure was over. When he gave David back to me and I started to put him on my breast, the *mohel* said he still had another chant in Hebrew. This final blessing gave him a Hebrew name, David Tzvi.

David was happy sucking on my finger and fell asleep into a deep slumber. He had slept most of the rest of the day in our sling or being held by William. The *mohel*, following tradition, gave the other boys Jewish names, too: Z'ev Yonatan to William, which means "wolf," and "G-d gave," and Simcha Alexander to Scott. Simcha means "happiness" and from the Greek origin Alexander means "helper of men." The older boys like their names. David means "beloved."

John thought it was the quickest circ he'd ever seen. John may not understand why this *bris* was important to me and it may seem odd to him that I would willingly have this religious ceremony in my home when I have always questioned faith. But I feel thankful for my three healthy sons, and I feel glad to have finally had a naming ceremony for all of them.

Ironically, it almost seems that the anti-circ movement showed me my reasons to have the *bris*. The movement (which also brashly claims that fulfilling this covenant is no longer necessary) was put before me so that I would understand that circumcision was not to be taken lightly and that the spiritual side of Judaism was an important part of my heritage. The *bris* was the finishing touch on my experience giving birth to David. Not only did it welcome David to the Jewish community, the ceremony spiritually kindled me. My only regret is that I did not have my camera handy to preserve the hallowed moment when the *mohel* held David up by the window to present him with a blessing.

TO MY SONS: HOW YOU WERE NAMED

Your Dad says that his parents, Irma and Guillermo Coquelet, had an obsession with naming all their boys "Guillermo." *Tata's* name is Guillermo Gregorio. They named their sons Juan Guillermo (your Dad), Guillermo Herman (your *Tio* Willie), and Eduardo Guillermo (*Tio* Eddie). Dad joked that he wanted to name all of his boys "Guillermo," too. He bothered me with this throughout all of my pregnancies. He also insisted that if I had a girl, we'd use the feminine form, Guillerimita. "No way!" I said.

William, Scott and David, this is how your names were chosen. First and most important, Dad and I had to like how your names sounded. We'd be the ones calling out your name and talking about you hundreds and hundreds of times. It seems like so many parents want the endorsement of family and friends on a given name. I didn't care if others thought you had a nice name. Your name needed to please us.

William John, your name was straightforward. "Guillermo" is the Latin form of "William." Your Pop-Pop's name is "William." In addition, I liked the sound of William. It's a solid name. It's simple. We decided early on, soon after we learned you were a boy. Both grandpas could be equally happy.

Your middle name is "John" for your Dad's American nickname. We could also call you "Guillermo Juan" to give you connection to your Latin heritage. In fun you're known around our house as "William the Conqueror" or "Willliam of Monarch." (Monarch is the name of a neighborhood we lived in when you were a baby.)

Scott Alexander, we tossed around a few more name ideas for you. We didn't name you until after your birth. Dad finally gave in. "You labored and birthed him," he said. "You can have the final say." We both liked the name "Alexander." Playing around, we came up with a nickname to call you: "Alexander the Great." You and your brother had names associated with well-liked kings in their time. Dad was hesitant about calling you "Scott." He wanted to know *who I named you after.* Your Latin name became Scot Alejandro.

David Stuart, we didn't know your gender until your birth. If you had been a girl, you would be "Rebecca Denise." We had an English, Greek, and could possibly have a Hebrew king (or matriarch) in our family. We couldn't initially think of a middle name for a boy. Old wives tales, and a few of my friends, said that you'd be a girl since we chose and agreed on a girl's full name. (Obviously they were wrong. Grandma Maxine doesn't have a middle name, though she always wished she did and insisted you have a middle name.)

We had to find you a middle name. The morning after you were born, the three friends that attended your birth were sitting with us, and the conversation turned to your name. William wanted you to be called "David John" like him. Then he moved on to think of other "J" names.

But then it dawned on me, "David Stuart." You were named after the place where you were conceived, where we wanted to go back to, and where our three friends were from. Nostalgically, you also have an uncle named Stuart. I said it out loud to all. Everyone repeated it, "David Stuart!" Your name, like your brothers', belongs to an accomplished person and was agreed upon in an instant.

David, your name doesn't have a Latin equivalent. When we want to address you in Spanish we'll pronounce your name with an accent "Dah·vēd Stoo·árt." However, the *mohel* that performed your *bris* told me the direct Hebrew translation, "David Tzvi." I liked the idea of a Hebrew name so much that we also gave your brothers Hebrew names at your *Brit Milah.*

My friend Laurie lives in Israel and studies Judaic history. Here's what she told me about the origin of your name. David is a direct biblical name without an explanation in the Hebrew Scriptures. The first time David comes up in the Bible is when Samuel goes to Yishai to find out which of his sons will be the king. The scriptural David already exists as a little boy by that point. The letters of your Hebrew name form another word, "*dod*," meaning beloved. Because of that, tradition says that David means Beloved.

William, you were given the Hebrew name "Z'ev Yonatan." The *mohel* told you that "Z'ev" meant wolf. It reminded Dad and me of the song, "Hungry Like the Wolf." How fitting for you! You liked that.

As for your middle name, Yonatan was the biblical David's best friend and brother-in-law. (How appropriate that you should be named as one of David's friends!) The name means "G-d gave."

Scott, your Hebrew name is Simcha Alexander. I learned from Laurie that Alexander was Macedonian. In Greek, the name means "helper of men." When he conquered the Middle East, Mesopotamia and much of Egypt, Alexander declared himself chief god and was obsessed with immortality. When he came to Jerusalem, he made an agreement with the religious leaders that they wouldn't have to change anything in the Jewish religion but they would start calling their children Alexander. That was about 330 BCE, so it's been a common Jewish name ever since.

The *mohel* explained that the reign of Alexander was associated with good times for Judea. Since "Scott" has no Jewish translation I was given a list of similar sounding names beginning with an "s." We chose "Simcha," which means "happiness." It also reminded you of Simba, the Lion King.

I never gave much thought about the meaning of your names, initially, but I am now glad that I have looked into it. It's been a wonderful way to make you aware of your rich cultural background, while building your sense of who you are.

UNEXPECTED BENEFITS OF BREASTFEEDING

I am often in awe about what my children can teach me. In trying to keep up with my six-year-old's inquiries about G-d, I found the book *Teaching Your Children about God*, by Rabbi David Wolpe. This book suggests questions to ask and activities to do with your child to nurture their spiritual growth and strengthen their faith.

One of the suggested activities is to stand in front of the mirror with your child and ask him, "What features did you get from dad, from mom, and which ones did you inherit from G-d?" My son William answered, "My hair and tan-color skin come from Dad. My brain comes from Mom."

William wasn't sure what he inherited from G-d, so I suggested to him that his bright eyes, big smile, and beauty marks are the sparkle from G-d. This made him so proud. He likes repeating games, especially when the rules get changed just a little. So this time I asked him which features I got from my mom and dad. "Oh, I get it," he thought for a moment and jumped ahead to answer the next question that he anticipated from me, "Your night-nights (what he calls breastfeeding) are from G-d."

It is my turn to be so proud of him. I am glad I have been able to nurse him long enough for him to have the memories and insight that he does. I never imagined that spiritual growth would be a benefit of birth, and now I was finding spiritual understanding through breastfeeding.

COMFORTABLE WITH MY BODY THROUGH BREASTFEEDING

Three-year-olds like to chatter and play games during their special nursing time. David holds his free palm up to my palm and takes a break from suckling to speak. "Look, Mom. My hand is almost as big as yours!" Next, he tries stretching out his legs the length of mine, "Look, my leg is almost as long as yours." I turned the game around, "David, but your little night-night is not as big as mine." In reply, he stood up, arched his back. And he took both hands and pinched the skin on his chest between his index and thumb and said, "Now it's a big night-night like you have."

~♥~

A newborn's range of vision is about nine inches: perfect for making eye contact while they nurse. I learned that a three year old sees clearly at this range, too. David demonstrated this as he learned to identify his own body parts during nursing sessions. He showed me his head, ears, eyes, eyebrows, and eyelashes. He also shows me where my facial features are. While he is at the breast, he sees something he doesn't have. He points to where my neck used to be and asks, "What's that?"

One of the older boys explained in his wisest tone of voice, "David, when you turn 40, you get a double chin."

I love those boys!

~❤~

Once after a La Leche League meeting, I was appreciating my sons, and asked the two elder boys, "Aren't we so lucky to have David, the little cutie, as a part of our family?"

My oldest son agrees, "Yeah Mom, it is good to have him, if you didn't your breasts would be all shriveled up by now."

~❤~

These little games are examples of more unexpected benefits. They remind me of how my mentor in Breastfeeding Medicine, Jack Newman MD, replies to a mom who asks if pumping milk to give in a bottle is equally as good. He says, "There is much more to breastfeeding than just the milk. My 3-year-old has demonstrated his agreement.

WORKING AND BREASTFEEDING

W hen I anticipated going back to work after William was born, I felt panicked about breastfeeding and pumping. However, once I actually started working again, the routine of pumping wasn't as dreadful as I had anticipated. Of course, finding appropriate childcare and leaving him behind were different issues, but keeping him breastfed was reasonably manageable. I decreased my hours to the low end of what's considered full-time, working 72 hours rather than 80 per two-week pay period.

Before I fully appreciated the value of breastfeeding my son, I sought help from a certified lactation consultant (IBCLC) at the hospital where I worked. I was not having any major supply or latch issues like so many women have prior to going to work.

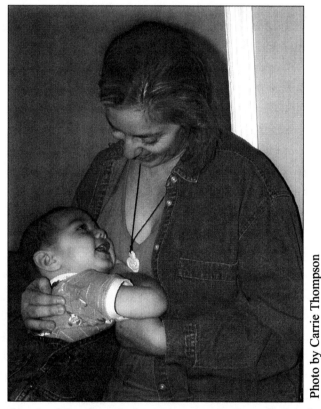
Photo by Carrie Thompson

It was just that I had purchased a double electric breast pump and needed help with it. She made a few helpful suggestions about pumping and recommended a different size flange that fit me better. With her help, I was quickly able to build up a frozen supply before I went back to work.

I wasn't an IBCLC then, and I didn't yet attend La Leche League meetings. Having contact with a knowledgeable person reaffirmed and fueled my determination to breastfeed. Not only was my commitment solidified, but also I was intrigued by the work of an IBCLC.

Although studies show that some women can manually pump as much milk with their hands as with an electric breast pump, I am not one of those women. Having a quality pump secured my success. Another issue was that I felt that I had to "warn" everyone at work and seek people's approval to pump. This turned out to be completely unnecessary. I worked 9 a.m. to 7 p.m., or thereafter, until the last patient was treated and discharged. Counting travel time, I averaged about 11 hours days, and sometimes more. I went back to work about 12 weeks postpartum.

I gave myself a few days to get in to a routine. Luckily, I quickly worked it out. The first day took the longest. I soon realized I could leave my pump set up in my office so I wasn't packing and unpacking it. In other words, I learned how not to waste time. I received a lot of unexpected encouragement from the staff. My success was important to them.

Very rarely, my son was brought to me at work during my shift. Babies figure out our schedules and accommodate us. They sleep more during the day and then nurse at night. This may be good for the sitter, but not so good for a tired, working mom.

During the first three months of work, when my son was three to six months old, I pumped my milk during my lunch break and later in the afternoon. My second break was usually during those downtimes when I'd be waiting around, anyway; for my nurse to bring my patients back, for lab results, x-rays, respiratory treatments and so forth. I could multi-task. I often returned patient phone calls or performed needed research while pumping. I could use one forearm to hold both flanges with practice. (I didn't yet know about set-ups for hands free pumping.)

If I could not get the second break before quitting time, I quickly pumped just before leaving. Even though it seemed that it might be better just to get home to nurse, five minutes of pumping maintained my milk supply and comfort and replaced my milk for the next day. The staff told me that despite my pumping, I kept up with the patient load and my "break" was often unnoticed.

I breastfed William just before leaving in the morning and started again the minute I arrived home. He had unrestricted access to my breasts when I was not at work. This kept up my milk supply while reconnecting and bonding.

When my son was more than six months old, I only pumped once during my shift and remained comfortable while replacing my milk. I was dedicated to my commitment to pump. William took 18-20 ounces while I was gone to work. I always had plenty of milk in the fridge. Each day he drank some of my freshly pumped milk and some of my frozen stored milk. The days I worked each week varied, but my body and milk production regulated to my schedule.

I pumped at work until William was 11 months old, but he continued to nurse well beyond the one-year mark. He nursed without restriction when I was home, and he slept in my bed so we could be together and get rest. I actually missed my quiet break at work.

When Scott was born, my pumping routine was on the same timetable. I went back to work at about three months, pumped twice a day until he was six months, stopped pumping after eleven months and continued to nurse beyond the first year. But there were some differences. The office closed at 5:00 p.m. now, so I got home sooner. I officially went part-time and was able to attend evening La Leche League meetings. Another difference was that I was tandem nursing. The milk flowed.

With both boys, I waited until breastfeeding was well established with no complications before letting my sitters introduce a bottle. There was no reason to train them ahead of time to suck from a bottle. My sitters used bottles for both William and Scott only in my absence. William would take any container holding any food, anytime, and it never interfered with nursing. Scott, on the other hand, never liked the bottle. He would stall his feeds for six or eight hours, until he was too hungry not to eat. He completely refused bottles after seven months.

Both of these patterns are common with breastfed babies of working mothers. I was lucky; some babies don't do so well switching between breast and bottle. I didn't know there were alternatives to bottles—like cups, syringes, or spoons—for feeding a baby. With my first son, I thought that he would need a bottle with a sitter for as long as he nursed. Not true. Both boys gave up bottles long before they gave up nursing, without any negative consequence.

Neither William nor Scott would take a pacifier. Little did I know then that a pacifier could have interfered with latch and milk supply or I would not have tried to give them one at all.

Seven years and a third baby later, I was an IBCLC, setting an example, and confidently giving new mothers permission to breastfeed. I wasn't working outside the home when David was born. I could bring him everywhere I went. It is with great pride that I can see that he only received breastmilk from the breast. David was never offered a bottle or a pacifier. I opened my practice when he was nine months old. It wasn't long before he could ask to stay home to play with his older brothers and go on junk food missions with his dad.

KIDS AT WORK WITH MOM

I n my new practice I found that my patients tolerated nine-month-old David's presence well. Some of my returning patients were glad to have the opportunity to meet him. I found other reasons to have my kids in the office. There have been times when my kids have calmed an upset child in the office faster than I ever could. The older boys have played with kids while I talked to their parents about adult concerns. Sometimes kids bring out the best in the person you least expect; I've seen a few of our disgruntled clientele cheered-up by a smiling baby (mine or someone else's). I have had acutely sick patients tell me they feel more relaxed in a medical atmosphere of kids and youth.

I nursed baby David in the office on demand, and I certainly think David has set an example for some mothers how to nurse better than my words could. David has been good at modeling sling use and promoting proper use. Having my baby around has given me a connection to establish a rapport with the new families I want to attract.

It got me thinking, "Why must a mother have to choose between outside employment (and leaving the baby), versus staying home?" I imagine returning to the work force sooner would have been easier on me if I had the flexibility of this third option—bringing my baby to work. That's why I'd like to propose a new support group called "Kids at Work with Mom" (KAWM). Just because "kids in the workplace" isn't the norm in our society doesn't mean it shouldn't be encouraged. In many countries, it is socially acceptable to have kids in the workplace.

But because I have done it and continue at times to try it, doesn't mean that it is always easy. Not all the traffic through the office is tolerant of my kids. It isn't always smooth with one or more kids demanding my time, distracting the staff, or making a mess. And as I have found out, like everything else in mothering, there is always someone to judge and criticize.

Certain phases of babyhood and childhood may actually be easier to deal with a young one in the office. For example, a newborn in a sling would likely be very content as opposed to a toddler which David was when I opened the office. Then finally they may reach a maturity where they may want to help and don't have to be supervised constantly.

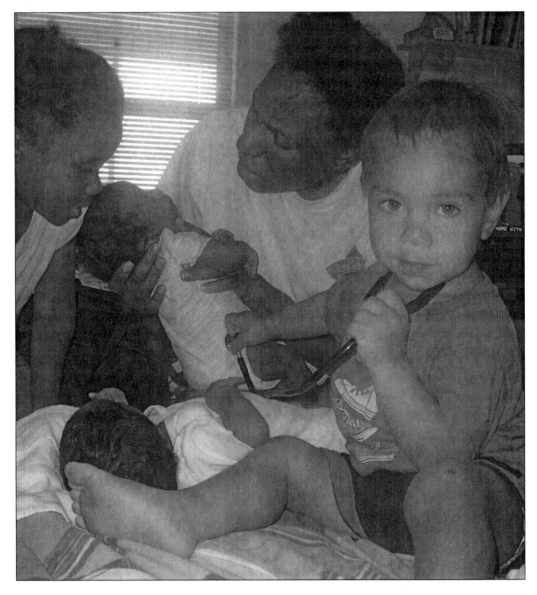

Three kids in the office at once is a lot. My kids are home most of the time. I will bring them all, last-minute, if a sitter is ill. But better yet, planning to bring one at a time on a half-day or home visit, after hours or on hospital rounds can benefit them;

it's important for kids to see what adults do.

Many years ago my employer "joked" about me bringing my first newborn to the office papoosed to my back. Of course then, I would have never dared do anything so out of the ordinary. This was before I really knew anything about wearing a baby and having a lifestyle where babies are a priority. Now, I couldn't imagine if I had another baby leaving him behind at home.

If it was an acceptable thing to do in our culture, we might have already come up with many good solutions to the problems we'd run into, like playrooms readily available in an office and child-friendly rooms for supplies, or bringing the sitter to work with us. Fortunately, I finally found on-line support groups promoting this kind of flexibility for the working mother.

HOMESCHOOLING: THE FIRST YEAR

"Homeschooling is so hard."
"How do you have the energy when you're pregnant?"
"How will you have the time with a breastfeeding baby in the house?"
"When do the boys socialize?"

These are things I frequently hear from people not familiar with homeschooling.

My first son, William, is a September baby. This is a bit eccentric, but at the time of his birth, I was cognizant of the fact that "my genius" missed the cutoff to kindergarten and would not be required to enter school until he was almost six. That was not going to do! There was also outside pressure to put him in a preschool by three months old so he wouldn't miss out on "the educational advantage of starting early."

My husband had other concerns; he was over-protective (not a bad thing in this case) and couldn't dare leave his *primogenito* under a strangers' care. It was just as well because preschool hours didn't seem to match our work schedules. In the meantime, I stocked up on brand-name reading and foreign-language curricula by the time he was 18 months old.

I don't recall when homeschooling became a conscious thing for me, but it wasn't long before I relaxed and realized that the world is a classroom and that I didn't need to be tied down to formal schedules or someone else's curriculum. By the first year we came under the homeschooling laws, we took advantage of this flexibility. And we also had the support of lots of homeschooling families to help keep perspective during times of outside criticism and questioning.

The first official year of homeschooling included moving out of state and traveling. I did not look for employment, and I savored my time with both boys, knowing that I would be back in the work force soon enough. Anticipation of a new baby has not been a hindrance to learning, and young boys don't need to be confined to desks. Nor do they need to be diagnosed with behavior disorders and controlled with meds in order to make a teacher happy.

If we had done nothing else that first year except move from Florida to Georgia, we would still have completed educational requirements for William, who was six years old that year. I was not legally required to document Scott's learning, because he was just four that year, but freedom from documentation didn't mean he wasn't learning.

Moving exposed us to a variety of subjects. The boys were introduced to geography through maps and compared their native coast terrain with the mountains of Georgia. We found elementary biology in regional plant and animal life. Our study of meteorology was enhanced by the fact that Georgia experiences all four seasons, which is very different from South Florida. William and Scott practiced rudimentary writing skills in the notes and photos they e-mailed to their friends, describing their new experiences. Every time we went back and forth from Georgia to Florida to visit our loved ones, they practiced their budding math skills: "How many months until we go back to Florida? How many miles is it to Georgia, and how much time will it take to get there?"

Besides the usual school subjects, my boys got to raise their EQ (emotional intelligence) as we processed all the feelings that go along with moving. It is stressful not only for adults but also to young children. And if you've ever moved you realize it takes much longer than you expect to process the grief of leaving friends behind. At the same time, learning how to face loss with the support of your family and healthy coping skills is probably the best lesson that anyone can learn in childhood.

~♥~

We went back to visit Florida three times during our first "school" year. Young children learn through repetition, and all of our "lessons" were reinforced with each trip. We have traveled elsewhere, too, in our homeschooling career, and that has presented a host of learning opportunities. Scott has been to Florida, Georgia, South Carolina, North Carolina, Virginia, Maryland, Washington, D.C., Alabama, Tennessee and Washington State. William has also been to Canada, Nevada and Arizona.

These trips have included beaches, mountains, state parks, jet skis, the Smithsonian, aquariums, hiking, barbecuing, mining, rock quarries, canyons, waterfalls, caves, ethnic restaurants and historical activities like Civil War re-enactments and Colonial craftsmanship.

Our adventures have also included the socialization that the under-informed worry so much about. (I can't help but remember every schoolteacher who ever said to me, "Turn around and face the front, young lady. We're not here to socialize," or "The quietest student gets a reward at the end of the week.") William says a trip is not a vacation unless you see your friends. Through homeschooling, he has learned the value of friends and real socialization. Scott says his favorite trip is to Grandma's to get toys.

To finish up their first "school" year, my sons attended a British soccer camp. Their coaches were from Wales and Scotland, and both boys still talk about those countries. They recognize their flags, and Scott even acquired a British accent.

When worried (or are they jealous?) people fret that kids might fall behind by moving out of a school district, I don't have to deal with that secret fear that they might be right. I know our boys were exposed to a tremendous variety of learning opportunities in the very first year of homeschooling, more opportunities than many school children will ever have!

UNSCHOOLING: THE SECOND YEAR

I t was time for the end-of-year homeschool evaluation for 8-year-old William and Scott, who is 7. It had been a stressful year. In some ways I questioned my decision to keep them home again, because it felt like a self-centered year for me. We had moved back to Florida after being out-of-town for 18 months. My husband and I opened our private practice in July. We were in the eye of two major hurricanes in September. Then I suffered the loss of my grandmother in December.

All of those events distracted me from carrying out a formal plan to educate these boys; I had to wing it most of the time. Since I work, I was also concerned about childcare: I had 23-month-old David to consider.

When we opened our practice in July the three boys often came to the office with me. My husband and I were at first busier with the administrative duties of setting up the office than seeing patients, so keeping them with us at the office worked for a while. As we picked up some patient volume, my husband and I split the days in half and took turns taking the older boys out of the office.

My youngest, David, stayed with me until he was walking and eating solids well, and until he indicated that he wanted to follow along with his brothers. I accomplished a major goal that I had as a working mom: David never had a bottle or a pacifier, and I kept him with me his first year.

As the practice got busier that first December, our Mondays filled up first. My housekeeper Mary, whom I had known for several years, offered to keep the boys with her on Mondays when she was at our house, anyway. Besides Dad and me, Mary was the first person that David stayed with. He was 14 months old.

Mary quickly became more like a nanny than a housekeeper. The boys took well to the idea of spending Mondays with her at home. Mary spoiled them with pizza and baking treats together. One-year-olds love the vacuum and brooms, while the older

boys love spraying. Mary seemed to know magically how to engross them in her routine. I could have never gotten them to help me around the house like that.

By December the older boys were getting invited to play dates just about when I need them to be more occupied outside the office, but David still hung out with me at the office. The play date turned into a quality Wednesday afternoon of play, swimming, board games, drawing and even a volcano experiment with their four friends!

By next April, Fridays were getting full in the office, so we asked the teens of another homeschool family to stay with the boys. William, Scott, and David thought of it like another play date. By May, David wanted to stay and play with all the kids on

Wednesdays and Fridays. He was 20 months old.

Eventually, Mary started staying on Tuesdays, which was my last day to fill. So their schedule became: Monday and Tuesday with Mary; Wednesday afternoon with our friend and her four kids; and Friday with homeschooled teens. I am generally with the boys on Wednesday mornings and all day Thursday.

Our office hours are 9-5, and I go home at lunch. Anyone who knows my homeschooling-supportive sitters think I have the best of all worlds, not to mention a blend of good people and resources to draw from. This variety gives the boys a wonderful opportunity for social and creative stimulation. I like how they are with kids of all ages and a variety of special needs (including Mary's daughter with Down syndrome). I like how they visit someone else's house on Wednesday.

During the month of January, I started panicking (again) because there was no structured learning. With all I had on my mind, I couldn't focus on teaching them anything that didn't come easy to them. I hired a tutor two to three times week to concentrate on reading and writing. Her rewards program incorporated some math in that they kept up with their points. After about four months William could read, and he would pick up books to read to his baby brother. Scott learned his letters.

We had lots of "electives," too. We stumbled across a Spanish tutor who came to the house once a week. William enjoyed this lesson.

The boys completed a year of Sunday morning Hebrew School and got awards for good attendance. They each were proud to be in a short class play. They made some great artwork. (My favorite craft was a paper mache puppet.) They baked ethnic snacks for the appropriate holidays and learned songs with their class.

Our homeschool had a full line-up of sports. Both of the older boys played in the homeschool soccer league that Fall. After that, William did Tae Kwon Do for a few months. Both boys enjoyed swimming, jet skiing, billiards and air hockey. They even got in a weekend of snow boarding. I enjoyed the flexible nature of these sports rather than being tied to a set team schedule. They often enjoyed these activities with their dad, which was good for all of them and gave me the chance to give David my undivided attention. For instance, William and Scott went on a "Man's Weekend" to North Carolina with Dad, Uncle Ed and Dad's friend "Lake Man." I managed to go on more local trips with them to Tarpon Springs and Key Largo.

The boys are my photography assistants, and I can really see their developing artistic sense. They both are good photographers themselves and have had their work published to accompany my articles.

Scott's crazy about animals. On his trips he looks for "new species." We have had a few overnight guests such as tadpoles, snails and salt-water crabs. We acquired pet hamsters, two hermit crabs live in our tub, and we have an ant observatory.

That second year, they saw three performances at the local theatre with a homeschool group. They attended British Soccer camp again, as well as two other camps with friends, making more crafts and learning music and yoga. I treasure the candles they made.

So my boys stayed busy and were learning all the time, but I still worried about all the time I spent on my needs, especially at the office, and wondered if the boys got their educational needs met. I worried about whether they will enter adulthood ready to face the future. Then one day, Scott said that he wanted to start a business, pass out business cards and make a website. I realized his goals are the same as mine, and they didn't come from an artificial or arbitrary curriculum. He is observing and learning from life, and his life's goals arise organically from that. I thoroughly enjoyed helping him build his website.

LIFETIME OF LEARNING

N ow my boys are 10, 8, and 3. They are independent and insist on having long hair. They watch a lot of TV and play interactive games on the Internet as much as they can get away with it. William is a strong reader, but says he doesn't like it. Scott remembers everything I read aloud to him, but he doesn't want to read it himself.

My youngest continues to nurse upon awaking in the morning, then again when I come home in the evening, and finally to fall asleep. He looks forward to nursing "wrapped in a towel" after his bath. I still come home at lunch, but at some point David stopped asking to nurse during my lunch break. Likewise, I don't really remember when the oldest boys completely weaned. Sometimes all the boys are so engrossed in their games that they hardly acknowledge I've come home.

When William weaned there was Scott still nursing and filling the void. When Scott weaned David was on the other breast. I'm sure I'll remember the details of David weaning, probably with much emotion. I've enjoyed the nursing years.

The struggle of accommodating a breastfeeding baby into my busy life is almost past. I've been lactating for over 10 years. Fortunately for me, David is unlikely to wean abruptly. He gives me a chance to accommodate gradually to life beyond the childbearing and breastfeeding years. I'll begin to accept that middle age is inevitable.

~♥~

William's the one that takes drum lessons, but all the boys bang on the drums, imitating the basic beats. One-two-three-four. A one-y and a two-y and a three-y and a four-y. One triplet, two triplet, three triplet. David imitates the drumbeat on my breasts using his palms and thinks he's real funny. The music instructor says William can skip over "high school band" lessons. I ask him to bypass contemporary music and teach him rock-n-roll rhythms.

Homeschool is accommodating. The boys have three hours of karate lessons a week and spar constantly at home, using their techniques with *nunchaku* (pronounced num-chucks) and other martial arts weapons. I depend on William to look up the spelling of these karate words for me.

We have a coastal boat this year. Our family has taken a few trips off both coasts of Florida, The boys learn a lot about boatmanship and marine life. We once towed in an elderly man whose fishing boat conked out. I could tell this man was getting concerned he'd be adrift in the dark. My boys had another perspective; they thought towing in a boat was the greatest adventure. They are goods swimmers and divers, both in the ocean and in the pool.

We tend not to go on faraway vacations with three young boys and a busy practice, but that's okay. I knew we wouldn't. We got it out of our system in prior years. Before marriage, I'd been to Alaska, I saw the glaciers and the Midnight Sun, the Grand Canyon and Grand Caymans. Being a mother is the most inspiring of all journeys.

They continue to use their heelys and hulahoops. Scott and David are particularly limber. They do gymnastics off of my dresser and onto the bed, or off the counter onto the couch. Such is life with three boys: it's not for the lighthearted. All my breakables have been packed and put away.

English lessons are stimulated by Mad Libs. William constantly reminds me that the correct way to pronounce "you" is "yu" and not "ya." And it's a potato and tomato, not a "potata" and "tomata" as I say. I don't know who taught him to enunciate so well.

They learn math through on-line community games. (I admit we let them play Runescape.) They have bank accounts and brief cases at home to keep up with valuables. Runescape is a "sin" in many homeschool households, but Scott is a millionaire on the game. To be rich, he must be learning some math!

William is great at Scrabble. Playing Scrabble with him shows me the true extent of his vocabulary. He writes Medieval action adventure stories using Microsoft Word. The apple didn't fall to far from the tree.

We've read biographies about inventors, pioneers, and geniuses like Washington, Lincoln, and Einstein. We proudly point out that these heroes were self-educated success stories.

Our new "Wednesday family" has tons of pets. They raise rats to feed their snake. The family had two iguanas for a while and a fish tank. There have been several litters of hamsters and kittens, stray cats and puppies. We've observed that human interference—even the mere scent of humans— can disrupt the nurture of a litter, even to the point of rejection. Does this disturbance by humans sound familiar?

The family found a stray kitten that they fed with a bottle. The kitten became weaker and weaker until, he rejected the bottle, not having strength to suck. Before they could get him to the vet, we thought to use a syringe to feed the kitten. We could just push milk in. No active sucking required. This reinforced a point I find myself saying a lot: There are effective ways to feed babies other than a bottle when a breast is not an option! This kitten regained its pep before seeing a vet.

My boys learn more than natural science with the Wednesday family. They do creative projects also. The boys made the cutest gingerbread house. I would have never had the patience to do that with them. I was so impressed; I took a photo of the boys with it for our holiday greeting card this year. The Wednesday family lives in a neighborhood with lots of kids. This is when they get to play outside with "neighborhood kids."

After many years, Mary is still their nanny, and Bernadette's homeschooled teens come over on Fridays. I have seen for myself how homeschool kids grow up to be responsible young adults that *I* can count on. We take advantage of all the talents each person in our lives has to offer.

If you look for educational opportunities they are out there. All the situations we encounter are potential learning experiences. This is the year we've learned more about eating nutritiously. The boys have learned about organic farming and preservatives. Scott still eats plenty of junk, but he has begun to ask if there are preservatives in the food he eats. I've noticed that his behavior has improved since making diet changes. And William has trimmed down. We've decreased David's cavity risk. I feel better overall; the food tastes better. Eating more produce leads to recycling and reusing. We slowly incorporate changes to better the environment and ourselves.

The schooling goes both ways. They teach me. For example, I didn't know my sons liked mushrooms. Each week I give my ration of mushrooms back to the organic co-op. One day I ask the boys, "What do you want for lunch?"

"Beef stroganoff, like Dad buys frozen."

I wonder, "What is beef stroganoff?" I put it into the search engine. I couldn't believe it was mushrooms. If they liked it frozen, they'd like it better fresh. I learned something about my boys that morning and we all learned how to prepare a new meal from scratch.

~♥~

I am self-centered again this year. I have work-related goals—treating patients, training staff, writing this book. Sometimes I think, "Maybe they should go to school?" But I notice that my own work and book writing skills encompasses subjects and areas that school never taught me. I spent 12 years in school *after* high school. My education provided me with the requirements to get my MD degree and licenses, but it was up to me to stay motivated and continue learning the things I really need to know to practice medicine well.

I think about all the things I've mastered—writing, my computer, photography, birth and breastfeeding. These are all skills I have taught myself, or that someone else taught me outside of the confines of school, because I have a passion for it and soaked it up easily. I wasn't a "straight-A" or "4.0" student like physicians are usually thought of. I did well with the sciences and philosophy. In English Composition, my grades were brought down for every grammatical error, despite my creativity. It left me afraid to write for years. (Fortunately, in real life, a writer can hire an editor to fix grammatical errors!)

I am grateful for my advisors in college and medical school admissions team who saw the person behind the grades. They saw my potential and encouraged me onward to medical school.

This is how I want learning to be for William, Scott, and David. I do not want to put my kids into school where they learn someone else's curriculum, burn out and then find they can't pursue their own interests because they've lost their passions.

And how do I educate my patients? When I see breastfeeding families for an office visit, I have less than an hour. Some I may never see again. I explain, "I can't teach you everything you need to know in a short visit about breastfeeding, but I can give you the resources to empower you to continue learning. And if I've done that, I've done my job. That way, you can get the most out of breastfeeding and parenting experience. It's the same with my boys. I don't arbitrarily control what they learn; I teach them how to learn—how to find out more about anything that sparks their interest. I teach them perseverance by letting them follow an interest all the way through, rather than switching to another subject every 30 minutes. Most of all, I've taught them that learning is not something separate that happens in a specialized setting at a certain time. Learning is life—ongoing and constantly changing.

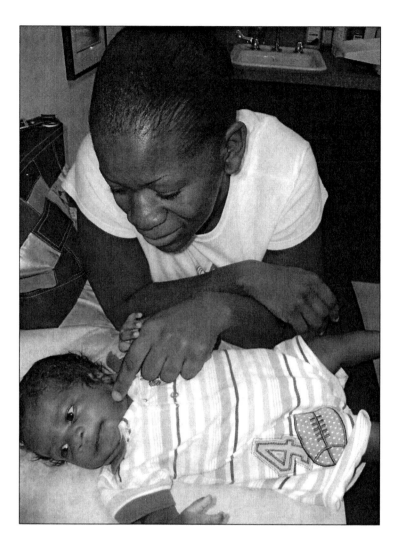

PART 3 - BREASTFEEDING MEDICINE:
MORE THAN PERMISSION

My son was going through a phase when he was not satisfied with the amount of milk I produced. "You know," I told him, "There is medication to take to increase the amount of milk."

"I do not want medication. Yuck!" But his eyes soon brightened when I explained that I would be the one taking the medicine.

What do you think is the first word that each of my sons could recognize by the time he was four years old? B-r-e-a-s-t-f-e-e-d-i-n-g!

"My soup is delicious, but my night-nights are good for me, too," claims David.

"What do you think of having all these babies in the house?"
I asked my 5-year-old nephew, a big brother for the second time.

"It's OK. Breastmilk is free."

William watched as I pumped some milk.
"Mom, the milk is so warm.
Why would anyone want warm milk?
It was cold when I was a baby, right?"

With a big grin, 3-year-old David, announces
his phone number:
"466-ninie-nights-ninie-nights"

BABY SHOWER GIFT

I recently made a trip to a department store to find a baby shower gift. The Mom already has a boy and a girl, and her nursery was set up. She probably has lots of stuff already, but everybody loves baby things. It should be easy to find something nice.

The first thing that caught my eye as I approached the baby section was a lovely table set up with piggy banks. Except that these banks weren't shaped like pigs at all: They were shaped like a bottle, and they were stuffed with smaller bottles and other trinkets that every baby "needs." As both a lactation consultant and a caring friend, I was not interested in anything that might undermine Mom's commitment to breastfeeding.

I moved on to the next table, full of diaper bags. Each bag had a matching bottle in the pocket. Then I looked over at the bibs. The first one that caught my eye was the one that said, "I love a full tummy." However, bottle icons were quilted all over this bib. I couldn't find one that said, "I love Mommy's milk." An alien (or just an inexperienced mother) visiting this store might think that a bottle is something a person must have prior to being born. I finally settled on a bib that said, "I love Mommy." Then I found a coordinating onesie and an outfit to match.

Bottle-feeding is so normal in our society no one ever stops to think about all the images of artificial feeding around us. I went to pay for my items. The clerk said, "Thank you for choosing our store today. For spending $30 you get a free bottle warmer and bottle."

"No, thanks. The baby will want to breastfeed."

She was surprised. "What about Dad? What about when Mom wants to get away?"

I explained to the clerk that Dad knows that breastfed babies have the advantages of bonding, protection against infection and a higher IQ than artificially fed babies.

Dad is willing to wait until the baby is ready for solids in a few months before feeding the baby. In the meantime, he will bathe and cuddle Baby often so he can bond.

Mom knows, I went on, that her baby wants her milk from her. She knows there are risks that come from introducing bottles early, even when those bottles are filled with pumped human milk. She knows that every baby has a different temperament. She will wait until her baby is born and is very comfortable with breastfeeding before deciding to separate herself from her baby.

For a first-time mom, I explained, I would give a gift such as a sling or a book like mine. Giving a bottle warmer undermines a mother's confidence to nourish her baby. Also, a lot of people feel obligated to use a gift just because they have it.

The stunned clerk asked, "Would you like to get a gift bag for your items?"

Glancing up at the rack of bags, I noticed the design on them: cartoon babies holding bottles. "No, thanks," I said.

No wonder breastfeeding rates are dismal. I could have gotten a few bottles in that trip without even intending to buy one in the first place. I finished my purchase and headed to the stationary store, wondering if I would find a card that depicted a loving mom cradling her baby, or would the cards also down play the importance of breastfeeding?

I have come to the conclusion the best baby shower gift is not a tangible one. It is not one that you can wrap in a box. The best gift I can give is to make sure that moms are prepared with accurate birth and breastfeeding information. I give the support they need to get breastfeeding off to a great start.

Your newborn won't care about the colors of the wall, the ruffles, the pattern on the bottle, or even the crib. The baby will not care how big the menagerie of stuffed toys is, or that everything matches. The best gift that a mother can give her child is the nurturing, warmth and better health that breastfeeding provides.

JUST SAY NO TO FORMULA COMPANY DIAPER BAGS

Formula company diaper bags are durable, cute, insulated, and just the right size for diapers, rags, changes of clothes, wallets and sunglasses. They are also "free," but they come with a huge price.

These corporate "gifts" are dangerous for the mom who wants to breastfeed, even the one called "Breastfeeding Success Pack."

First of all, these bags contain ready-made formula in bottles. All you have to do for the first serving is screw on the nipple, feed the baby and toss it out when you are done. The company makes it very easy. There is no powder to mix in that first sample, no water to sterilize, no measuring and no washing. Which is all very tempting when nursing isn't going so well at first, and you are exhausted.

After having four ounces of formula poured into her tiny tummy, your baby is full from the heavy meal and sleeps for a nice long stretch. Parents can rest, too. Everyone is happy.

Bottle-feeding seems easy, until you get engorged. Or after a few days of supplements your milk supply dwindles. Then you can say, "I tried to breastfeed, but I got mastitis," or "I couldn't make enough milk to keep my baby happy." Then you'll spend about a thousand dollars the first year on formula and bottles that need to be prepared, measured, heated, washed, and stored.

Secondly, who are you going to go to for help when you have breastfeeding questions? Surely not the office or hospital that gave you that bag? Do you know how they got those bags to begin with? They got them by talking to the formula company salesman, who wants to sell his product. The rep's priority is not to promote breastfeeding. It is to convince the consumer that formula is equivalent to breastmilk and to make breastfeeding sound complicated. He wants to present formula as an equivalent choice when nursing isn't going well.

But say you are committed to breastfeeding and that you tossed out the formula. You just want to use that bag because it is so cute and will keep your water cool. This is a contradiction. As a breastfeeding mother, you would be advertising for formula. You are glamorizing the formula industry. These bags are a successful marketing strategy to get you to do their work, which is to advertise breastmilk substitutes. These companies know you will use that bag for two years or more.

Look and notice all the mothers using one of those bags. You will carry that bag everywhere you go. Other people will view you with your bag and perceive bottle-feeding as normal. That's what the formula companies want.

So don't let yourself be tempted to use formula or get sucked into advertising for formula manufacturers. When you are handed one of these promotional "gifts," just say **NO**.

IS IT WORTH NURSING MY NEWBORN ALL NIGHT?

Q: My two-week-old breastfed baby is not sleeping through the night. Should I start cereal or formula in a bottle to help him sleep through the night?

A: First, I would like to congratulate you on your decision to breastfeed. The colostrum, the first milk you have provided for your baby, is specifically suited to meet your newborn's needs. Simply put, it protects your newborn against infection with a concentrated form of antibodies, white blood cells, and ant-inflammatory factors. The first milk helps your baby transition from the womb, where he had all his needs met around the clock, to a world that expects babies to feed on a schedule.

The American Academy of Pediatrics states that breastfeeding is the preferred feeding method. "Exclusive breastfeeding is sufficient to support optimal growth and development for approximately the first six months ... Breastfeeding should be continued for at least the first year of life and beyond for as long as mutually desired.... There is no upper limit to the duration ...and no evidence of psychologic or developmental harm from breastfeeding into the third year of life or longer."

The U.S. Surgeon General recommends that babies be fed with breastmilk only — no formula — for the first six months of life. It is better to breastfeed for six months and best to breastfeed for 12 months, or for as long as you and your baby wish. Solid foods can be introduced when the baby is six months old, while you continue to breastfeed.

The well-documented benefits of breastfeeding included decreased gastrointestinal and respiratory infections, including ear infections; decreased incidence of allergy; reduced frequency of certain diseases later in life, including breast cancer, osteoporosis, diabetes, ulcerative colitis, Crohn's disease, and obesity. Children who were breastfed as babies also tend to score higher on standardized intellectual achievement tests.

Try some of these suggestions to get your baby to sleep longer at night: Give a warm bath in the evening. We all feel refreshed after a bath or shower. Sleep with your baby. This way you don't have to get up for feeds. You can nurse in a side-lying position and fall asleep together. Often babies may wake up to be comforted and know your presence. Your baby may sleep better knowing you are close by.

Solid food like cereal should never be put into a bottle at any age. Bottles are for liquids and any solid particles like cereal can cause choking.

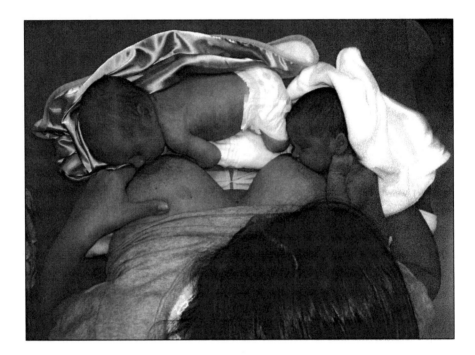

How Dads (and Grandparents) Can Show Support

Dad and other family members want to bond with the newest member of the family but may not know how to go about it. Here are some ideas for beginning your new relationship while supporting Moms effort to breastfeed.

Try a bath. Bring baby right into the tub or shower with you. Skin-to-skin touch is a great way to relax together. The sound of flowing water has a calming effect.

Burping is a favorite. Men especially seem to get great satisfaction out of eliciting burps.

Nap with Baby. You may benefit from the rest and Baby will have the security of constant contact, just like in the womb, and may even sleep more soundly.

Wear Baby in a sling. This is a great way to enjoy your precious little one that leaves your hands free. Baby can and should be involved in your activities.

Take Baby to the rocking chair. Some of our favorite family photos show Baby asleep on Grandfather's shoulder.

Play airplane. Lie on your back and hold Baby by the torso. Lift baby like a wriggly weight. Babies practice head control in this horizontal, face down position. They also get a different perspective while you strengthen your pecs.

Sing, talk and shake rattles. Babies quickly learn to follow both familiar and new noises. You can see your baby develop better eye and then head control almost daily. How proud you'll be when your young baby turns upon hearing your voice.

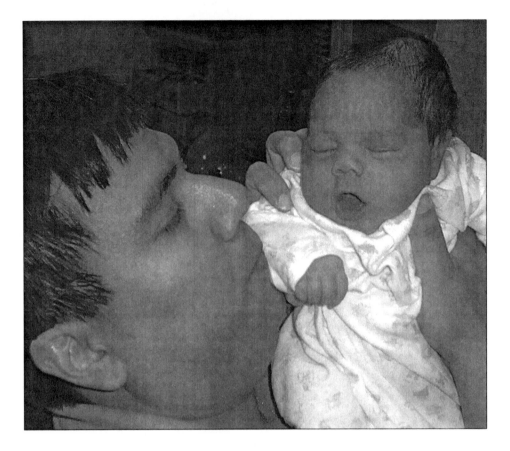

Most babies like a variety of sensory experiences. Rub a soft blanket on the skin, massage in lotion or comb baby's hair.

I also have a couple of thoughts on what may work against bonding.

First, don't supplement feedings *just* for the experience. Baby needs mother's milk and it is best straight from the breast. Mother needs Dad's full support. Each baby has a unique temperament and just one supplement can potentially do a lot of harm. Instead, let Dad or other family members give Baby her first taste of solid food *after* six months of age. This "delayed gratification" will have tremendous health and psychosocial benefits to Baby. If supportive relatives have concerns that Baby isn't getting enough to eat at the breast *do* help by locating a specialist in lactation.

Second, don't leave all the diaper changing to Dad. Men often perceive this as a chore. Dads deserve to relax, bond and have fun with Baby.

"I COULD NOT BREASTFEED BECAUSE…"

"I could not breastfeed because…"
I had previous breast surgery
I was expecting twins
I'm too small
My nipple is inverted
My baby was premature
I had weight-loss surgery

"I did not breastfeed as long as I wanted to because…"
My nipples and breasts were sore
My baby had jaundice
I needed antibiotics
I suffer depression and/or chronic pain
My baby did not gain weight
My baby gained too much weight
My baby wasn't satisfied
My baby was allergic to my milk

Unfortunately, mothers express these regrets too often. These myths are especially sad because none of them are valid reasons not to breastfeed. With the proper support, *all* of these barriers to breastfeeding can be handled. A good place to start getting that support is at your local Le Leche League meeting.

If you read this in time, attend LLL meetings before your baby is born. At a meeting you will have a chance to discuss your concerns with other moms. You will also have a chance to see babies breastfeeding. That's important because most new moms have never even *seen* breastfeeding.

Specific medical concerns can be discussed with an International Board Certified Lactation Consultant, a health professional that specializes in breastfeeding. It would be worth finding out if there is a physician that specializes in breastfeeding in your area. Fellow Le Leche League members may know some, or you can ask your hospital or prenatal care provider to help you locate one. Also, a doula can be with you to get breastfeeding off to an optimal start within the first hour of your baby's life. It pays to be prepared. Babies thrive on human milk.

SARAH'S THYROID

Photo by Sarah Perrie

As an "MD IBCLC," I'm both a breastfeeding advocate and a breastfeeding clinician. All these years, I have advocated the need for increased breastfeeding rates. Going into private practice was a big step. Anyone can give information and say "do this," but I wondered whether I could *really* make a difference clinically when mothers had some genuine medical concerns. When Sarah showed up a few weeks into my new practice, I thought, "Can I actually help this woman meet her goals!"

Sarah came to me with concerns about the safety of breastfeeding while on medications for Grave's disease (hyperthyroid). Several medications for thyroid are approved for breastfeeding mothers by the American Academy of Pediatrics, and Sarah's disease had been controlled with one of the safe medications for a few years.

Recently, though, the "safe" medication had caused a life-threatening drop in

Sarah's white blood cell count. So she had discontinued the medication, and now her thyroid was overactive. Her options were limited to a medication that I had very little data about, a concentrated solution of iodine.

When I researched it further, I received contradictory advice within the international lactation community. Even lactation specialists discouraged the use of this medication in infants, but, Jack Newman MD, always confident that breast is best, provided me with reassurance. Her surgeon eventually prescribed it

So we forged a new path. Since Sarah's 6-month-old, was no longer an "infant," and since the prescription was a short-term medication preparing her for surgery, Sarah decided to continue breastfeeding. We checked both the drug levels in mother's breastmilk and the baby's thyroid levels once a week for the three weeks that Sarah was on the medication. The baby's blood test remained normal throughout this process. The iodine did show up in the breastmilk in small quantities, but since iodine is also in formula, that was no reason to discontinue breastfeeding.

After three weeks of treatment on the iodine medication, Sarah's thyroid and blood count were stable, and she had her thyroid removed. Thyroid surgery is compatible with breastfeeding, as is most surgery, but the anesthesiologist warned Sarah not to breastfeed for 24 hours following surgery. He mistakenly assumed that anesthetics are harmful to a nursing baby. It is rare that a mother who is sedated has to interrupt breastfeeding. Many anesthesiologists will tell a mom to "pump and dump." The truth is that mothers can breastfeed post-surgery as soon as they are wake. By the time a mother is awake enough to breastfeed, the meds have already been cleared from her body. This is well documented in research studies. Sarah recovered well and her baby remained very healthy, too.

FAILURE TO THRIVE

I met a mother and her 6-week-old baby out in the community. As I was admiring this breastfed baby, I noticed he was on the morbidly thin side. I questioned the weight and learned that he had not yet regained his birth weight.

Failure to thrive is one of the most worrisome things I see. It is not always easily identifiable unless you actually weigh the baby or know what to look for. We just take for granted that babies grow, and even thin babies may have dimples on their thighs and have the wrinkled-up look.

The mom brought the baby into my office the next day. Back in my medical training days, I would have panicked and immediately given formula and IV fluids. Plus, we would look for disease by doing a lot of invasive testing. We'd probably have admitted the baby to the hospital to feed him and watch him gain weight.

With my interest in lactation, I take another approach. It made sense to me to evaluate milk transfer first. I had the advantage of meeting this mom out in the community. I knew her extended family and knew she had support. I didn't think she was purposely starving her baby. The baby was not dehydrated, either, so I knew I didn't have to use formula or IV immediately. After getting a medical history and exam on both mother and baby, I knew it was unlikely that any disease caused the low weight.

I observed the mother breastfeeding and thought the baby just wasn't getting enough in. We adjusted position and latch and talked about how to get more high fat milk into the baby by a breast compression technique. I advised her to nurse all the time including at night, side by side. I discouraged pacifiers, because they result in non-nutritive sucking.

Mother had the baby weighed three days later. Things had turned around quickly. After a few more weeks, he continued to grow and thrive without artificial milk or supplements. The mother's milk supply was adequate, and her baby was spared much invasive testing.

Since, I've had several more "failure to thrive" graduates younger than six weeks old. Some are easy to fix. With just a few adjustments in breastfeeding technique, the baby grows quickly again.

Other times it seems like I can't find anything wrong. My guidelines say the breastfed babies should regain their birth weight by two weeks, but some regain that weight more slowly and yet the babies seem normal.

Of course, other times, I find that the mother has insufficient milk supply. I must find the cause and work within the mother's potential. It's important to get the support of a lactation consultant anytime weight gain is slow.

NOT ENOUGH MILK?

I had to give Jen bad news. "Your pituitary doesn't send the right signals to your milk-producing glands. You won't have enough breastmilk to breastfeed." I had found a subtle abnormality in her hormone work-up. But Jen proved me wrong—Not enough milk doesn't mean you can't exclusively keep the baby at the breast.

"The Lact-Aid is working great! I actually have nursed the baby while lying in bed! It has been nice as nursing is not feeling as restrictive as before. I very much like the positioning of the system... I can use it as is without having to tape tubing all over my breasts as I had been doing with the other system...He took to the Lact-Aid right away...

"The only down side to this is that he doesn't have to suck very hard at

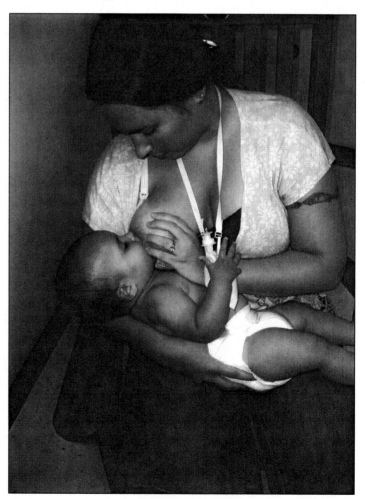

181

all … which may be the proper way to nurse for most... I have been trying to nurse for a little while before giving him the supplement but many times he is very impatient. The only time I can really do this and he gets a good portion of breastmilk is during his early morning feed when my breasts are very full (a wonderful feeling I wish I could duplicate more throughout the day).

"He is doing a lot of comfort nursing... lots of times he insists on this to go to sleep so I am sure he is getting a little then. I am trying to keep up with the pumping but it is very time-consuming and hard to get to as the baby is awake more of the day…Some days I can pump four or five times a day and then other days I never really get to it. But I figure it is more important to cuddle and play with the baby rather than put him down to use the breast pump. The only bad thing is I notice a definite decrease in supply if I slack off on the pumping.

"Maintaining the system is not too bad. At first glance it did seem like a lot of parts and upkeep, and you need a wrench, but it is no worse than what we had before. After figuring out how to disassemble to sterilize before the first use it is a breeze. You just have to be careful because there are some small parts that you wouldn't want to loose down the drain!

"I am enjoying my breastfeeding experience way beyond what I could have ever hoped for. I am glad I didn't give up!"

NURSING AN ADOPTED BABY

J udy called the office. "I'm planning on adopting an abandoned baby. I can't get pregnant because I have polycystic ovary disease. My OB won't prescribe me the meds I'll need to induce lactation. I didn't know who else to call. Finally an IBCLC from WIC told me about you. Can I make an appointment?"

I quickly printed the protocols for induced lactation before Judy came in. I was ready to explain them to her. But Judy was informed and educated. She already had the protocols printed and in hand when she came in. She knew exactly what prescriptions she wanted: oral birth control pills, prescription galactogogues and Metformin. There are also herbs that help bring in a milk supply, and she was already familiar with them. She has a hospital grade electric pump and was ready to follow the protocol.

Judy is expecting to have a baby within a month, so she'll follow the accelerated protocol. She'll also use a supplemental system at the breast until her milk supply builds up.

DONATING HUMAN MILK

Kym breastfed all of her own four children. She offered to provide her pumped breastmilk to the mother of the surrogate baby she now carried, but the mother was successful at inducing lactation for a full milk supply.

Kym offered her milk to her friend, Lisa, who was pregnant and due at the same time as the surrogate baby. Lisa had a breast reduction in her early 20's and was concerned that she might not develop an adequate milk supply for her little one. Way before delivery, Lisa prepared to optimize her own supply but also gratefully accepted Kym's offer. Kym underwent a complete battery of infectious disease testing to ensure the safety of her milk, and she was happy to do it. "There will be a non-formula option available for Lisa's baby!"

Lisa provided Kym with an electric breast pump, shipping supplies and purchased a large freezer for storing the milk. Because the two women shared a similar due date, coordinating age appropriate milk was possible.

After delivery, Lisa discovered she could only provide a small portion of her baby's milk requirement. Kym continued on prenatal vitamins and focused on eating a nutritionally sound, healthy diet and started a dedicated pumping schedule resulting in a full milk supply. Kym's generosity and dedication allowed Lisa's baby to be fed 100% breastmilk.

~❤~

I am a 200 ounce breastmilk donor to the Human Milk Banking Association of North America, HMBANA, the only non-profit milk banking organization. At the time that I had excess breastmilk, I didn't personally know anyone who needed it. I always thought it would be gratifying to know someone who needed my extra milk that plumped up my newborns quickly.

After Scott was born, both William and Scott nursed a lot. When I returned to work with the breast pump, I easily expressed up to 40 ounces of milk during the two breaks of my 10-hour shift. Scott was the only one I was pumping for; William ate solids in my absence. Then Scott reversed his nursing cycle; that is, he waited till I came home in the evening and nursed more throughout the night. The pumped milk in the freezer accumulated fast.

I decided to donate my excess milk to HMBANA. I was screened and cleared to donate by my midwife. My baby was also screened to assure the organization that he didn't need the extra breastmilk. Once I got the go-ahead, the milk bank sent cylindrical four-ounce containers for storage and a shipping cooler with directions for keeping my milk frozen while it was sent by air overnight. It's an amazing process.

ALL IN A DAY'S WORK

A mom came in with her 2-week-old son, desperate for breastfeeding support. She had been bottle-feeding expressed breastmilk for a week because of sore nipples and breasts. She had gone through the same thing with her first son, and she'd given up breastfeeding by two weeks. She didn't want to give up breastfeeding with this baby. This mom faced a whole list of problems:

1. She had nipple wounds on her right breast. The breast was not too tender at this point, since she has been giving her nipples a rest from breastfeeding. We corrected position and latch, and Baby latched right on. I prescribed nipple ointment and comfort gel.

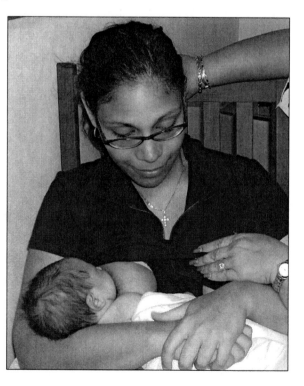

2. There was mastitis of the left breast. I had her continue the Doxycycline she began with her last doctor. She continued to feed or pump to drain that breast frequently.

3. She had been bottle-feeding for a week. With proper positioning and latch baby took to the breast. He also nursed well in a ring sling, which I showed her how to use.

4. She was disappointed, because she'd had a repeat Cesarean in giving birth to this baby. I gave her some support information and resources.

5. Her breast pump flange was causing breast pain. The problem was that the flange was the wrong size for her. We fitted her with the correct size to solve this.

6. She was concerned about returning to work. We talked about how the priority was to let all wounds and infections heal and become comfortable with breastfeeding. Then we could focus on preparing for work. I encouraged her to feed the baby directly from the breast, although she could pump for comfort and store that milk for when she starts work. I also prescribed Le Leche League meetings.

7. Elevated blood pressure was another issue. Fortunately, I could treat her blood pressure while maintaining lactation.

8. This mother showed symptoms of postpartum depression, which was understandable with all the above contributing. I allowed her to express her feelings and grieve the loss of a vaginal birth. If her symptoms did not resolve, I would have had her follow up to address the depression specifically.

At the end of this visit, Mom admitted that she'd been afraid to come see me. She had thought that I would tell her it was hopeless to breastfeed and instruct her to quit. Two days after she came into my office, she was much more satisfied with how breastfeeding was going. She was still getting shooting pains in both breasts. I treated her for ductal thrush with Diflucan and Probiotics, and she was able to continue breastfeeding. Her mood improved tremendously once nursing was going well.

This woman's experience just goes to show that most "obstacles" to breastfeeding can be overcome or prevented. Don't be afraid to get help early from someone knowledgeable about breastfeeding. It's not hopeless: Help is available!

BREASTFEEDING AND BIRTH CONTROL

Barbara's breastfeeding is going well. Her OB wants to insert an IUD at her six week check-up. Susan said her OB will only give her the mini-pill. Rhonda said her OB wanted to give her a shot of Depo right after her baby was born.

For women who exclusively breastfeed and have not resumed having a menstrual period, breastfeeding is an excellent form of birth control for the first six months of a new baby's life. However, women are often not presented with this option. I can remember being told in my training, "Breastfeeding is good birth control for the population, but not for the individual." Over and over women are indoctrinated, "If you don't use prescription birth control you will get pregnant." As a result, physicians give "individuals" birth control out of fear that another pregnancy may occur. Birth control is not without side effects including potential compromise to milk supply. Amenorrhea is a pleasant benefit for many exclusively breastfeeding mother. The hurry to make a non-cycling women cycle without careful counseling is disturbing. I have never understood the rush for OB's to prescribe birth control. Birth is good for their business!

Ecologic breastfeeding is good birth control for women who are instructed properly. I also find that women who enjoy breastfeeding usually enjoy mothering more and want more babies eventually. I encourage women to learn more about lactational amenorrhea, child spacing, and natural family planning. The Couple to Couple League International offers information, books and classes.

FREEING THE INFANT TONGUE

My second son was born with ankyloglossia, more commonly known as tongue-tie. When Scott arrived I didn't know much about this minor congenital defect. My son's cry simply caught my attention. I looked and saw that his tongue was held back by a piece of tissue in the midline underneath his tongue. In medical-speak, this piece of tissue is called a sublingual frenulum.

When Scott tried to move his tongue forward, the tissue held his tongue down, making his tongue look notched or "heart-shaped" at the tip and wide-based laterally. I didn't like the looks of it and wanted something done. I asked the postpartum nurse if she knew anything about it. "That's a tight frenulum," she explained, "but no one does anything about them anymore."

Because I was fresh out of residency and had never encountered any discussion on newborn frenula, I believed her. But I wasn't satisfied and kept asking around. The hospital lactation consultant was familiar with the breast-feeding problems a tight frenulum can cause. I wasn't having a nursing problem, but I still wanted my son's tongue released. In retrospect, breastfeeding was not a problem for him because my milk supply was well established by William, who was then 22 months old. All Scott had to do was open wide, and the milk poured in!

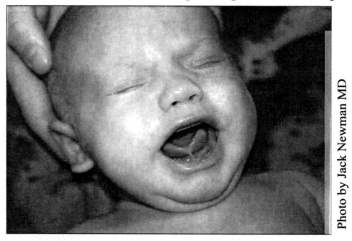

Photo by Jack Newman MD

I asked an ear, nose and throat doctor I trusted about releasing this tissue, and he was willing to do it. The lactation consultant thought I was lucky to get my needs resolved. The postpartum nurse had been right in saying that physicians generally don't treat tight frenula. In fact, there is a huge void in resources to help babies who are having breastfeeding problems because of a tight frenulum. It concerned me that it was easier to get the frenulum released for cosmetic reasons than for greater ease and success with breastfeeding.

My baby was scheduled to have his frenulum clipped in day surgery with a small dose of mask anesthesia. I thought this a bit much. I had a notion that I should just do this at home with a scissor, but being a vulnerable postpartum patient, I went along with the medical protocol. At the last minute we found out that day surgery didn't take babies under a year, so we were delayed a few weeks and rescheduled for the operating room.

The OR required the formality of a hospital admission, so we admitted my little 6-week-old to Pediatrics and obtained blood work from him. The OR procedure also required NPO status "to prevent aspiration." All this for a tight frenulum really did seem like overkill!

The procedure my son *actually* had was a z-plasty. A frenotomy is a simple snip with scissors of a thin membrane, but my son's surgeon actually cut into the base of the tongue, realigned and put in a stitch. The procedure was very brief.

As the months passed, I was surprised to hear how many babies had a tight frenulum, which created breastfeeding problems and often weaning in the first week of life! I learned how hard it was to find providers to snip the frenulum. When I researched the references current at the time I found that most of these babies need just a simple cut (with curved Iris scissors) of this transparent tissue.

The first office frenotomy I performed was on a physician's baby. I told him about the research I had studied, including the highly recommended "how-to" video by Evelyn Jain, MD, IBCLC. He watched the movie and agreed that this didn't seem to be a major operation. Like me, he wasn't interested in doing a procedure on his own baby. His wife was reporting breastfeeding problems, and the release helped. Their family had a history of tongue-tie, which is common. In our case, we could trace it to my father-in-law.

While, in theory, there is no pain for the baby, it can be an uncomfortable thing to be held down and have your tongue pulled out. I find that simply swaddling the baby in a receiving blanket is sufficient restraint for this procedure. If the baby cries, it actually puts the tongue in the best position for cutting the frenulum. No infection or life-threatening bleeding after a frenotomy has been reported, but I am required as a health care provider to warn parents of potential for bleeding, infection and even death in any procedure. Parents must sign a routine consent form.

I explain, "The breastmilk will provide anti-infective properties, and the action of breastfeeding will apply appropriate pressure to stop bleeding." Professionals who respect lactation will let the baby nurse immediately after the snip. There is no NPO before the office procedure, either. In my professional experience, the most blood I have seen is one controlled drop, the size of a pearl, under the tongue after a snip. In some cases I have seen no blood and I second guess whether I had actually cut the tissue.

I keep benzocaine gel in the office in case the baby needs an anesthetic, although I prefer not to use it. In a young baby with breastfeeding problems, an anesthetic can make it even more difficult for the baby to nurse. Thus, I would not be able to assess the latch and transfer of milk afterwards.

Some conservative sources indicate that if the frenulum is nontransparent or you can see structures like blood vessels, this is a contraindication to frenotomy. But experienced providers have ways to handle this. While I have cut through some tissue somewhat thicker than my protocols state, I have not seen any extra bleeding or other complications. Time, more experience, more case reports of safety from frenotomy providers and a more relaxed legal community may redefine contraindications.

I have also released a few frenula only to observe tight bands hidden underneath. Sometimes I have snipped deeper and sometimes not. Reducing the obvious one is a good start and may be all that is needed to improve breastfeeding. A referral to an ENT or oral surgeon can always be made to release the tighter, thicker bands if breastfeeding problems continue.

Does all tongue-tie cause breastfeeding problems? Probably not, but another risk of not doing a frenotomy is the potential for speech problems. Try talking while holding your tongue down at the base of your mouth! Brian Palmer, DDS, is also concerned about cavities and occlusion and sleep apnea. A tongue free to move involuntarily sweeps the gums and teeth, freeing food particles. Without this tongue lateralization, cavities are more likely. A tight frenulum also puts pressure on the gums and developing teeth, making the need for braces more likely.

Is a frenotomy a panacea to correct breastfeeding problems? No, a few babies needed further referral to oral motor therapy. A delay in doing the frenotomy may compound the condition, leading to a cascade of problems including weak suck, poor milk supply, mastitis and so on. I would prefer to do them as soon as the need is identified, as soon as possible after birth.

SECOND OPINION ON JAUNDICE

Angela, with tears, brings her three-day-old baby in for a second opinion. Her friend referred her after Angela's pediatrician handed her a sample of formula prepackaged in a volufeed and insisted that the baby take it. He also wants to re-admit the baby to the hospital to treat jaundice in the nursery under the phototherapy lights. The pediatrician doesn't want to worry all weekend that the bilirubin levels *may* rise.

Angela wants to know what alternative treatment plans are available. She is correct in thinking that "this 'just-in-case' plan *will* interfere with bonding and breastfeeding." Angela brings in a copy of the report; the total and direct bili levels are elevated at 16 and 2, respectively. The pediatrician ordered other blood tests to eliminate jaundice secondary to blood type incompatibilities.

High bilirubin levels can lead to brain damage. That's what the pediatrician is concerned about; however, Angela's baby is nowhere near that critical level. The pediatrician is partly correct; increasing food intake will help the jaundice. But the pediatrician is wrong for not addressing how breastfeeding is going before introducing formula. It would have been wise for him to request a lactation consult. Since the levels are high, but still safe, I turn my attention to evaluate the feed and make adjustments to optimize breastfeeding. At once, I discover a tongue-tie that needs to be clipped and the "crisis" is easily put behind us as intake is immediately improved. If the quantity of Angela's milk had been low or the effectiveness of the baby's suckle had been poor, I could show her how to use a supplemental feeding system. She *can* and *should* keep the baby at her breast.

Assuming, we now have a sound feeding plan, the next step is considering whether lights are necessary or not. Indirect sunlight is a great way to get effective light therapy. One midwife says, "I have all new moms put the baby in the direct sun for five minutes on each side before 10 am and after 4 pm daily. The babies seem to love it and it really helps with the jaundice so common in breastfed babies."

If the weather is cloudy or there is concern that the baby needs longer durations of light, outpatient phototherapy lights can be rented. Angela can bring these lights home with her. Follow-up bili levels can be drawn at an outpatient lab over the weekend and results can be called to the physician, In this case, called to me. Perhaps it is less stressful on the busy pediatrician to go ahead and admit the baby, trust the nurse's report, and not worry about all the details of the feeds, rentals, and getting the blood results. Angela's baby has been spared a hospital admission and all the disruption that goes along with separation.

HOW LONG BEFORE SUPPLEMENTING A NEWBORN?

A 36-hour-old baby was referred to me by his midwife. The child had been born at home, had not yet nursed well and now had a fever. "Should I just send him to the Emergency Room?" I wondered.

Voices from my past intoned, "All newborns with fevers need to be worked up and observed in the nursery." I assessed the baby. He had good color and looked well. Mom had tested negative for GBS and other vaginal infections. She was un-medicated during birth.

I told the voices to hush, because they didn't fit the prototype of a hospital patient. The fever was resolved by undressing the baby. The baby was acting normal otherwise. This young women's psychological adjustment to motherhood was going well. There was good evidence of bonding demonstrated with skin-to-skin, eye contact, and a loving maternal voice.

The baby's mom was the oldest of 10 children. All she knew was breastfeeding and babies. Full-term babies are born with reserve. Knowing I was probably the only "pediatrician" in 3,000 mile radius that would, I sighed, and I calmly offered reassurance. She could observe him at home and call me at anytime. I felt confident he would nurse at his own pace. By the next day he was nursing just fine. This infant set the record in my practice for being the one with the longest time a healthy newborn took to initiate nursing. Babies sometimes just need a little time!

FIRST LATCH AT SIX WEEKS

I met Colton when he was six weeks old, just a few days before he breastfed for the first time. I had met his mother prior to this pregnancy and again early in her prenatal care. She breastfed her first son and attended La Leche League meetings. She knew without question that breastfeeding *was* the only feeding option.

Colton was born after a premature labor at 35 weeks gestation. He immediately had respiratory distress; therefore he was unable to coordinate his suckling with breathing. He was transferred to a South Florida Neonatal Intensive Care Unit and ended up on a lung bypass machine. He was fed his mother's expressed breastmilk by a G-Tube, a tube that went right through his skin into his stomach. She was able to pump enough milk to meet all his needs. His breathing eventually stabilized.

After a few weeks, Colton could breathe on his own, but he was not allowed to swallow, so he couldn't nurse. The doctors feared that if he swallowed he would choke and stop breathing. He was diagnosed with developmental delay attributed to strokes (cerebral palsy) that he suffered during his poor transition to life outside the womb.

Colton's mom brought him to my office shortly after he came home to show me how he fed. She pointed out that he was already developing contractures in his hands, and he did not support his head well. She was instructed to give him a pacifier while she poured the milk into the G-tube so that "his facial muscles would have a chance to develop." A pacifier was something that she never thought she would *want* or *need,* but now her son was therapeutically dependent on it. She kept him in her arms, alternating sides, breastfeeding style, while maintaining eye contact as she "fed" him. She was told to feed him every three hours. Like many breastfed babies he showed hunger signs sooner than three hours. Now out of the NICU, she could feed him per the tube on demand.

She explained to me how they determined he couldn't nurse directly from the breast. He had a swallow study called video fluoroscopy. For the procedure, he fed from a bottle filled with dye and the fluoroscopy camera was used to see if he could swallow without refluxing and subsequent choking. The test showed that he refluxed on the dye. Mom was strictly warned that she had better not give him anything by mouth or he would turn blue and stop breathing.

Upon hospital discharge she was given suction equipment. In case he couldn't handle his own secretions, she'd be able to clear his throat with it. She told me that she actually never needed it. She also told me that she has tried dipping his pacifier in her expressed milk so he could have the pleasure of tasting milk's sweetness. He never choked on the small drops of milk. She longed to bring her new baby to her bare breast. So her big question was, "Can I put him to breast? Will he <u>really</u> choke? Will he be able to first latch after six weeks?"

The mechanics of swallowing from a bottle are different than the mechanics of suckling at the breast, I reasoned. Bottle-feeding uses different muscles than breastfeeding. How valid are test results using a bottle when a baby has never bottle-fed?

So we made a plan. Mom would come to the office and pump her breast empty. Then she would put Colton to her nipple and see if he would latch. At six-weeks old, he did latch for the first time, and he did suckle, and he *did not* choke. In fact, he did quite well. He looked content being the breast as if he'd been there all along.

At home, Colton continued to receive his breastmilk via the G-tube. Every few days, his mom would comfort him by nursing on an empty breast. She took it, slowly; concerned that he might suffer with silent respiratory symptoms. He developed a cold, and she was very worried that he might aspirate into his lungs. He never did, though, and Mom continued the feeds. I'm sure the breastmilk antibodies protected him from getting a worse cold, just like it protects any other baby.

Gradually, Colton's mom increased the frequency of nursing and the amount of time on the breast. Within three months Colton was getting all his milk directly from the breast! This whole time she was very "hush-hush" about his breastfeeding.

At three months Colton was scheduled to have a follow-up video fluoroscopy swallow-study, to see if he could handle feeding by mouth. Afterward, his mom e-mailed me the news that he passed his test. Colton couldn't nurse lying down, due to nasal aspiration, but he could breastfeed as long as he tucked his chin in. When she "confessed" to breastfeeding him, she learned that nursing him had probably helped him pass his test!

Since those early days, Colton's family has moved out-of-state to be closer to a children's hospital with the specialists he needs. I still get e-mail updates that tell me Colton is *doing well because he continues to nurse*. I can just imagine Colton saying, "Thank you, Mom, for your determination to breastfeed me."

ANOTHER NICU GRADUATE

Lisa Marie's baby was admitted into the NICU for observation and stabilization after preterm labor at 32 weeks. Lisa Marie lives close to the NICU, and went as often as she could to see her baby during visitation hours. Her other three kids were breastfed, and she was pumping milk for this baby. Her goal was Kangaroo Mother Care, which is skin-to-skin contact (chest to chest) and exclusive breastfeeding. Evidence (and common sense) shows that this type of nurturing is especially beneficial to a preemie.

This NICU, like many, still follows old protocols that state that preemies need rest to grow (i.e., should be left in an incubator) and bottle-feeding (even mother's milk). They wrongly conclude bottle-feeding burns fewer calories than breastfeeding. I've had a NICU nurse there admit *to me* she is all for breastfeeding, "but doesn't want to handle mother's milk." For her, it's a relief when she doesn't have to expose herself to breastmilk. (Why is she a baby nurse?)

Lisa Marie said she certainly felt like her baby was stolen from her and felt undermined in being obliged to so many protocols. She did as they asked and hoped that with good feeding (even from a bottle) and weight gain she could get her baby out of there faster. Most babies from this NICU never get to the breast after discharge—too much harm is done. But Lisa Marie was experienced and committed as Colton's mother, so there was no other choice.

When Lisa Marie brought her baby in to my office for the first consult, she had a lot of questions about what she was instructed to do with her baby at home.

In the hospital nursery, the baby had reflux (and vomiting), so they put the baby on Zantac. My assumption was that the formula was to blame for the "reflux." Now that she was exclusively breastfeeding, I instructed her to stop the Zantac. The reflux never did come back again. It reminded me of long ago in "my" nursery, many of the babies were prescribed Zantac. We thought it was the cure. Little did we guess that

breastmilk was the way to go; increased breastfeeding should always be the first line of treatment for "reflux" in babies fed artificially.

Lisa Marie's baby was also sent home with an apnea machine—a monitor that is worn and goes off when there is a long pause in the breathing. Apnea is common in preemies. It may be very important in some families to use this machine continuously, because the baby gets set down alone, but Lisa Marie carried her baby in a sling all day long. She slept with her baby. She or her spouse was always there watching the baby. They would see for themselves if their baby had any pause in breathing. I gave Lisa Marie the go ahead to unhook the monitor while she was holding the baby (another benefit of babywearing). They did use the monitor at night when both parents were asleep, but there were never any more apnea episodes. Over time Lisa Marie became confident she could discontinue the use of the monitor altogether.

Since she had been diagnosed with apnea at the hospital, the neonatologist recommended follow up with a pediatric pulmonologist (lung doctor). Lisa Marie went to one visit (a two hour drive) and she reports the only recommendation was to come back every two months for an immunization to RSV, a viral infection that causes breathing problems in the winter months.

Over the years, I have observed how mild RSV is in exclusively breastfed babies. Like many recommendations in pediatrics, this recommendation was based on the pattern of RSV progression in babies getting formula without the antibiotic protection of breastmilk. The only caveat to make me think twice was that Lisa Marie's baby was a preemie. As it turned out, by four months old this baby was big and healthy, still exclusively breastfed. You'd never know she was premature. I felt confident allowing Lisa Marie to make a decision to discontinue the pulmonary visits. Any wheezing and congestion the baby experienced was mild and easily treated. We didn't need to refer out to a respiratory specialist.

Believe it or not, there was another specialist involved in this case—an orthopedist. This baby was diagnosed with "congenital hip dysplasia." Mom was instructed to keep the baby in a soft harness to keep the hips in proper position. What ever happened to double diapering? Lisa Marie kept the harness on for the treatment duration, but was so happy that I introduced her to cloth diapers for all the other benefits.

A POSITIVE PKU

Rita told me about her daughter, whose breastfed baby had been diagnosed with galactosemia via the PKU, the heel stick test required in every state. Galactosemia is an error of metabolism in which the body cannot transform galactose-1-phosphate into glucose-1-phosphate as it should. This condition is genetic and occurs in 1:50,000 live births. If not diagnosed and treated within the newborn period, it can result in death within a few weeks.

This baby was thriving. Mother was instructed to stop breastfeeding immediately when the gal test came back positive, because babies with Classic Galactosemia can't process their milk due to this metabolic birth defect. However, she pumped to keep her milk supply until all confirmation tests were complete, in case her baby has a variant called Duartes Galactomsemia.

Duartes Galactosemia has several degrees and expression, and these allow for varying amounts of breastmilk in the infant's diet. As it turned out, this was the type of galactosemia that Rita's grandbaby has. She learned that she could provide a moderate amount of breastmilk (along with soy-based supplement) and then have her baby tested every month. Soy-based formula was eventually eliminated from the baby's diet and they went back to exclusive breastfeeding.

By sharing this scenario, Rita has given me a model to go by. My goal when consulted by parents of babies with positive PKU test is to understand and interpret the test results in a way to minimize the disruption to the breastfeeding relationship.

SCREENING TESTS: NOT WORTH TRIPLE THE TROUBLE

My 37-year-old friend in Israel was 19 weeks pregnant with her second child. She shared by e-mail the bad news that her triple screen showed an increased risk for Down syndrome. She had repeated the test and was awaiting results. She couldn't decide whether or not to pursue amniocentesis. I replied to her e-mail:

Laurie,

Getting a positive triple screen result is devastating, isn't it? I did the test to appease my husband with my last pregnancy. He said I could have a homebirth as long as we did a triple screen to be sure our baby was OK. I gave in to get him off my back about the birth. I took it lightly, assuming the test would be normal. It turned out to be positive for Down's and Spina bifida. My son, David, is a healthy one-year-old now. Obviously my crisis is in the past, but it put a damper on my pregnancy and a strain on my marriage at the time.

Being confronted with a positive screening test makes you think about your values. It tears you apart from inside as you decide if you should repeat the triple screen, do the amnio, just have an ultrasound, wait it out or anticipate the possibility of life with a high-needs child. I chose to put it out of my mind. I never repeated the test. I did my best to enjoy the beauty of pregnancy. I sought out "anti-triple screen" opinions to remind me of how frequent false positives are and how misleading the test is. And I hardly told a soul. I chose to live with silent waiting rather than submit to what popular culture would pressure me to do.

I believe that Post Traumatic Stress Disorders exist and that I would have to deal with the consequences of "post traumatic abortion syndrome," even for a so-called medical abortion. I found no comfort in knowing that Judaism allows termination of pregnancy for severe genetic conditions. Who was I to decide if this was "severe" enough to count? I loved the baby growing inside me, and I found solace in believing that this baby was the right baby for me, no matter what.

Although some parents could not imagine living with the "burden" of a Down's or Spina bifida baby, I am not sure I could ever face a parent raising a child with Down's if I chose to terminate. Our nanny Mary had a daughter with non-diagnosed Down syndrome when she was only 24. Misty, her daughter, is now thirty-three. Mary, now a widow, shares, "I am glad I didn't know. I tried to conceive for years.

She was my only pregnancy. If I had known, I may have been pressured to abort. Misty is all I have now. I can't imagine life without her."

Another mom I know from Georgia had an amniocentesis that indicated her baby had a trisomy 18. Her daughter was born prematurely with an isolated heart defect and no chromosome syndrome. The heart defect had been confirmed by prenatal ultrasound. In fact, the ultrasound had indicated that all the characteristics of the birth defects this baby was supposed to have were present. The mother continued her pregnancy with this negative forecast. I can't imagine her surprise when she found out at birth that the chromosome problem was limited to the placenta. Had she trusted the amniocentesis result and the advice of the mainstream, she would have been pressured to abort (totally out of the question for her) a healthy baby.

I can't recommend the triple screen. Many women have it done with routine pregnancy labs without knowing they are being screened. Some think the test is diagnostic. But it only screens for risk. Furthermore, this test happens to be wrong a large majority of the time. My biggest fear wasn't the outcome; it was submitting to the cascade of interventions that would ensue if other problems with my pregnancy were found. I am glad I was strong and did not do any more testing.

Many moms tell me they wouldn't have just waited it out like I did. But I knew if I avoided the cascade of interventions, I would be OK, and even better off. Good thing. If I had known David was breech, I would have worried about that, too, and I wouldn't have had a vaginal birth, along with all the incredible personal growth his birth offered me. More intervention would have meant more diagnoses. "They" over-diagnose abnormal fetal growth, too much fluid, too little fluid and placental insufficiency, all of which leads to more worries, more intervention, more risk, more fear, more prematurity, more cesarean.

Amnio is not without risk either. Miscarriage is the most common; I saw this firsthand as a medical student. Infection, hemorrhage, amniotic leak and injury to the fetus are also risks. In addition, not all mental retardation or other congenital concerns are detected by amniocentesis. Telling parents their amniocentesis and ultrasound are normal gives false reassurance. After an abnormal amniocentesis result, often the only treatment offered by the medical community is termination. Someone for whom this is not an option has no reason to do an amnio. And there would be no reason to do the triple screen in the first place.

The medical community routinely recommends amniocentesis for women 35 years old and over. Many insurance companies pay for it without question. Families falsely assume that because insurance pays for it, it must be important. Being over 35 does increase your risk, but only slightly. After the age of 40 the risk increases more

211

exponentially. Still, it is just a risk, not a guarantee. (Mary was 24.) Many women have normal babies at 37 years of age—even in their forties.

Think of reasons why the triple screen might be off. Twins? High blood glucose levels? Or, most likely, your dates? Looking back, I think my dates were two weeks off. You said you were certain about your dates, but I was certain about mine, too. Somehow I must have missed a week. Are your weight and age and other data entered correctly on the lab requisition? Also, some labs report a narrower range of what is normal than others for fear of litigation if they miss one baby with a true defect.

I do realize that not everyone has a healthy baby, but I am not sure I would have wanted to know while I was pregnant. My husband said, "Well, at least we can know what to expect and be prepared." But my midwife said that, for the most part, she would not do anything different knowing the baby had Down's or Spina bifida. If there were a severe cardiac defect, the hospital would have resources. But I still wanted to birth at home in a peaceful environment. I could always go to the hospital afterwards, if necessary. If my baby was so critically ill that he couldn't survive an hour without heroic efforts, I would still be better off at home letting nature take its own course.

Repeating the test may seem like a good idea, but if the result is normal this time, are you going to breathe a sigh of relief? Alternatively, if it still shows increased risk, you will be more likely to pursue further testing and deal with the cascade of interventions that follows. If I had another pregnancy, I would not do the triple screen, and I would still refuse routine ultrasound.

Your friend in Florida,
Denise

NURSING WITH TEETH? AT NIGHT?

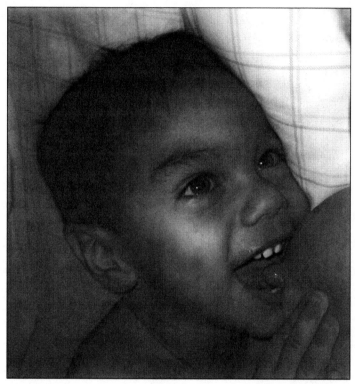

Going to the dentist for cleanings every six months is just a part of our lives. LLL recommends going within six months of the first teeth erupting. This preventive care hopefully lays the foundation for our dental health for the rest of our lives. The recommendation applies for all babies regardless of feeding method. I emphasize that breastfed babies are not exempt from meticulous dental hygiene. In my breastfeeding-skewed practice, I find more dental disease in breastfed toddlers than I see ear infections.

One of my moms, who survived multiple breastfeeding challenges to this point, was now upset after her 15 month old daughter's visit to the dentist. Because her toddler had tooth decay, the pediatric dentist said she must stop breastfeeding at night.

I shared my sons' dental history.

My first son has no dental problems. My second son who is eight years old now had staining on his front baby teeth. The stains were there when they grew in. The family dentist reassured me that they were just superficial and that his teeth were solid without decay. When he was about three, he could sit still long enough for the stains to be filed out. Neither of my two older boys had any major dental work. Subsequently there was no reason to discuss night nursing and our family dentist never told me to wean.

It is my third son with all the dental problems. His teeth grew in looking bad. At first I didn't think much of it because they looked like the stains his older brother had on his front teeth. But his stains got bigger and the tips of his teeth disintegrated. Of all my sons, he was the latest to start solids and he never had a bottle (because he was with me at work). He was actually the one who was more likely to sleep through the night (or perhaps I just slept right through the nursing).

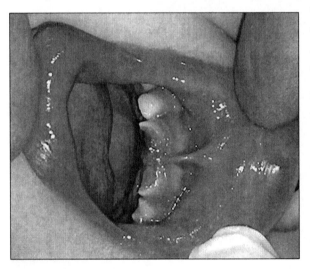

through the nursing). I suppose I was in a sort of denial that his front teeth needed work, "Not my breastfed baby!" His teeth looked really bad by the time he had them repaired. He was one- and-a-half.

Fortunately, there is a minimally invasive pediatric dentist in town with five sons of his own who feels that breastfeeding is important to a toddler's well-being. He will treat the decay and respect your right to continue breastfeeding. My son was sedated and caps were placed on his four upper front teeth. The dentist encourages good brushing, xylitol supplements, and nutrition (less sugar) as a part of the treatment program. Flouride treatment is individualized.

Our local La Leche League network helped me understand that breastfeeding through the night is entirely normal behavior for a toddler. If you stop breastfeeding at night, what beverage can you give that is healthier? Don't necessarily expect any baby to sleep through the night at this age. They are not neurologically programmed for that. In fact, nursing at night is one of the best things for neurological and brain development. Formula and heavy foods may disrupt this built-in, sleep-hunger-wake-feed cycle. If it's important to you that your breastfed baby sleeps through the night, and he does, count yourself lucky.

If you have a toddler without dental problems you may get away with going to any dentist you want because breastfeeding won't be an issue. If you have a breastfeeding toddler with caries, it becomes much more crucial to go to a breastfeeding-friendly dentist.

By the way, many moms give up breastfeeding when the first teeth show. "Teeth" should not cause breastfeeding pain. Consider other causes of "biting" such as nipple infection which should be treated. Actual biting could possibly be from "nipple confusion" where babies want to bite on moms like they do a rubber teat. That pacifier (or occasional bottle) that seemed harmless until now is to be blamed. This kind of nipple confusion can be prevented by avoiding rubber teats in the first place. Other times the biting may be a temporary phase the baby is going through. With a little perseverance from mom this behavior will end.

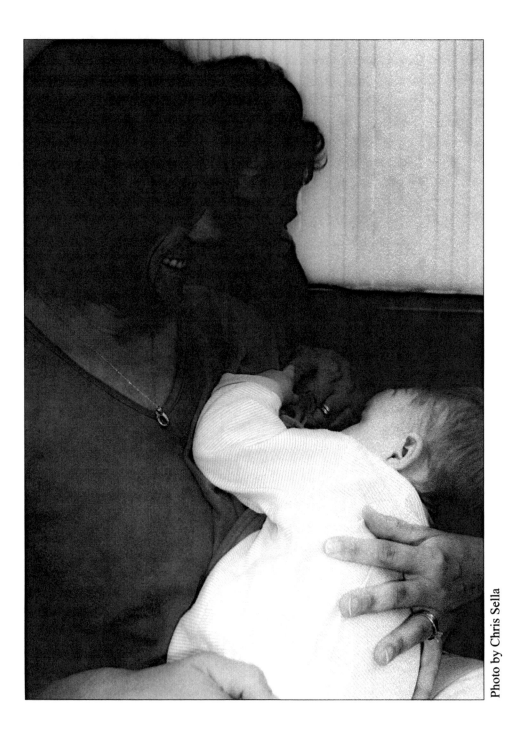

Photo by Chris Sella

PERMISSION TO GRIEVE

Trisha came back to my practice at three months postpartum. During the past year she had gone to her OB for all her care. A respiratory infection brought her to see me. Her three-month-old was now in the hospital with pneumonia. She had breastfed her first three children and it didn't work out for this fourth baby. Looking around my office at nursing moms and babies, and all the photos in my office, triggered her feelings about not being able to nurse this child.

I asked her to update me on the events of her pregnancy and birth. She said the birth was horrible. Her baby came quickly, but the placenta wouldn't come out. They massaged her abdomen to encourage the placenta to separate. She said the placenta finally separated and she bled. She was treated for hemorrhage. That she could put behind her, but then her newborn wasn't satisfied at the breast and wouldn't stay latched. The postpartum home health nursed suggested a nipple shield. I usually find that nipple shields are suggested before an adequate feeding assessment can be done. This was one such situation.

Trisha continued to have trouble feeding him that first week. Then she got re-admitted to the hospital for more bleeding and had a D & C. So innocently she told me they found *retained placenta*. NOW, I understood why all the feeding difficulties. I asked her, "And did your breasts start feeling full after that?"

"Yes, but it was too late. My mother fed him while I was in the hospital for three days. He loved the nipple and wouldn't go back to my breast. I miss not being able to nurse him so much. I take him in the bath and hold his body close to my skin, it feels so good. The pediatrician didn't understand why I was so upset about not being able to breastfeed. He told me, "Kids do fine on formula.""

I let Trisha continue to express her regrets. I find that when allowed to, many moms will express feelings of loss when breastfeeding does not work out. I asked her why she hadn't come to me. "I was tired, ashamed, and embarrassed," she said. (I silently wondered if her partner didn't support her breastfeeding efforts.) After she got it out of her system, I asked her if her baby lost weight the first week. "Yes, it was terrible!"

"Trisha, that first week you still had your placenta inside." She understood where

217

I was going with this…. "My body thought I was still pregnant!" "Yes, your breasts don't release milk until the entire placenta separates. That's why your baby was so fussy at the breast. He wasn't getting anything. He took the bottle, not because he preferred the nipple over you, but because he was starving. The shield they offered you wouldn't have provided milk, either. You and your baby are not incompetent at breastfeeding. The retained placenta was inhibiting your milk from coming in."

Breastfeeding Medicine includes helping women cope with such loss. I hope I helped her to accept this lost time. Having breastfed the first three babies, she probably realized that he may have avoided a serious respiratory illness like pneumonia, with the antibody protection breastmilk provides.

Another mom suffered lactation failure due to severely under-treated hypothyroid. She, too, grieved the loss of her milk supply, but when I diagnosed that the hypothyroid was a major factor to her breastfeeding outcome, she felt like a weight was lifted. It was too late for this baby, but she was pregnant with the next, and she had hope again.

For Trisha and her son, though, it was not too late. I informed her that some women re-lactate when they understand the reasons lactation failed. I warned her it would take commitment and work. In the meantime, I encouraged her to continue to provide the skin-to-skin time in the bath. That bonding time was still important. I also showed her how to use the sling to encourage more closeness throughout the day. I'm glad she came in and could process the first postpartum week in a new way.

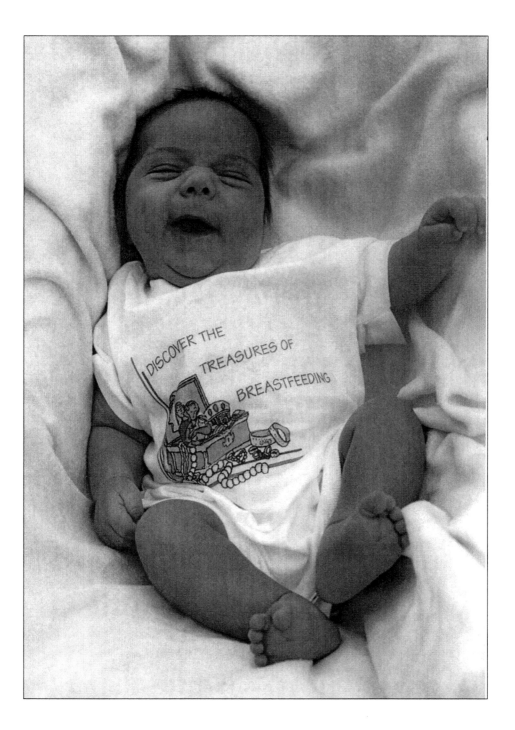

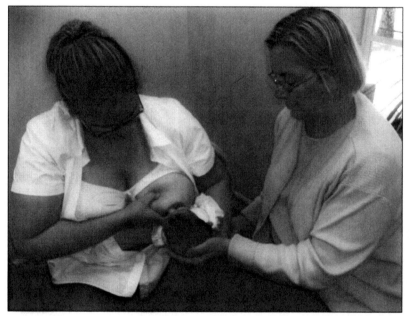

Photo by Scott Coquelet, age 8

Part 4 – Why I Do the Work I Do

I told then 4-year-old William that I was going on the Internet. Then I realized that I always say that I am going to use the computer and I asked him, "Do you know what 'Internet' means?" "Of course, Mom," he answers, "It's where you go to learn how to breastfeed."

I am responding to e-mail from my patients late at night. My son comes in and asks for night-nights. "Just a minute,"
He gets upset and throws a tantrum on the floor, "I don't want to wait just a minute. I want you off, now!!"
I hate to delay him anymore, but knowing I will fall asleep if I lay down to nurse him. I say, "Let me brush my teeth and get some water." I finally get to the bed. Where is William? I call for him. I look for him. I find him with his dad on MY computer playing airplane games.
"Hey, Dad, we tricked her!! She is off the computer. We can play now."

As a breastfeeding educator I often remind new parents that their babies nurse for many reasons in addition to hunger. Some of the top reasons my boys have given for wanting to nurse are:
I want to be warm and cozy.
I want to be like a baby.
I just love Mama's milk.
I am tired.
It will make me feel better.
I have a boo-boo.
It's like chocolate milk!

These are examples of the feedback I receive from my breastfeeding families. I share these letters because they convey the typical struggles of a family committed to breastfeeding.

BREASTFEEDING HELP IS AVAILABLE

"Our family just wanted to say thank you for going way above and beyond anything we ever expected from a family doctor. Without you I probably would have given up on my breastfeeding mission days ago not only out of hopelessness and frustration but also due to the lack of knowledge that there is help available. Until we stumbled into your office our understanding of breastfeeding was that you either have the knack or you don't—a belief I think a lot of new moms unfortunately share.

"I always feel such relief when we leave after a visit at your office because it reassures me that it isn't my capabilities as a mother that I lack but rather it is a lack in knowledge and support available to women. From the time our baby was born every step of the way has seemed like a roadblock to a successful breastfeeding relationship with our child—whether it was discouragement from hospital staff, information that never made its way to us, or even a total disregard of our wishes to strictly breastfeed breastmilk from other medical professionals! All in all we owe you a great deal of gratitude…"

–Jen C.

BABY GOALS I WANTED TO MEET

"Where should I begin? This past week was one of the toughest in my life. I didn't know what to expect and I had certain baby 'goals' I wanted to meet. When they didn't occur, I began to feel down. I thought I was incompetent ... I was crying and not sleeping. Definitely not a good combination. My mother-in-law decided to call La Leche League after I had kept putting it off. I didn't think there was anyone out there who would listen to my crying day and night. My poor husband. Then my mother-in-law said that someone had contacted her immediately ... it seemed a little too good to be true. I was instructed to call your office ... and they asked me to come right away! My husband turned around and picked me up ... and in your office, our baby nursed all by herself for the first time! We were tired and disappointed that she had to go to the ER the day before. After getting to be in your relaxed atmosphere of

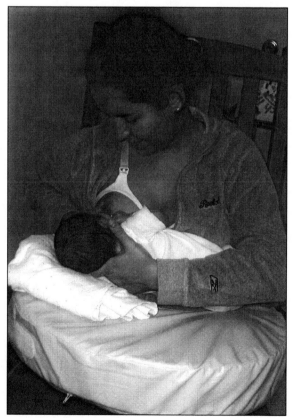

an office and being around someone who believed that I could do it … my frown really did turn upside down and from that afternoon on, I wasn't weepy anymore! Anyway, all that to say that I am really thankful for your care and you're listening ears."

–Catalina B.

Strengthening My Inner Confidence

"I just wanted to thank you for all of your help on Wednesday. I am amazed at what a remarkable woman you are. I cannot believe how much I relate to some of the things I have read on your website. I am so happy that I have found you. I know that when I came in I had a list that went in one too many directions... I had taken Katelyn to a sleep specialist. Looking back, I know this was a terrible mistake. He labeled Katelyn with a behavioral problem and that she needed to be left to cry in her room the week we were getting a hurricane. I am so glad that I didn't listen. I have continued to listen to that maternal voice deep within myself despite outside forces. I want to thank you for strengthening my inner confidence. It is hard to stay on a path that everyone tells you is wrong. I amazingly have continued to stay strong in my beliefs. I will be going to some of the LLL and ICAN meetings. I just wanted to thank you for opening up a brand new light for me. It is nice to know that there are many people out there that feel the same as I do."

–Amie S.

WORTH THE DRIVE

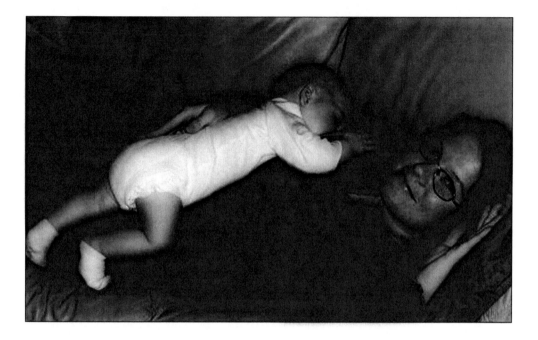

"I was just thinking about all the troubles I had at the beginning with breastfeeding (sore nipples, thrush, milk insufficiency) and how I am so happy that I stuck with it. I am really enjoying my breastfeeding relationship with my daughter now (even with two bottom teeth and two on the top coming in!) and I know that I probably would not be breastfeeding today if it weren't for you fixing her tongue-tie! The Ped's and ENT's around here said it didn't affect breastfeeding (ha!) but they would be happy to fix it under general anesthesia, which I did not feel comfortable with. It was worth a 1½-hour drive."

–Kristen N.

PUTTING ME AT EASE

"I called to make an appointment with Dr. Punger. It was her day off and she came in to see me. I was so emotional. Nothing was going right for me. Both nipples were sore and I had a bilateral mastitis. Dr. Punger put me at ease from the moment I met her. I unloaded everything on her. I often wonder if she's has seen anyone like me. But I felt comfortable with her from the start. We talked about my problems, from the breastfeeding to the vaginal disfigurement, to my depression. She spent a good hour and a half with me. Come to find out that we lived in the same neighborhood. She even came over later that night to check on me. Sometimes you'll meet someone that will touch your life and change your way of thinking. I found this to be true when I met Dr. Punger. I knew that I was so blessed to find her. My daughter will be a healthier person because of Dr. Punger."

–Shannon M.

A SENSITIVE TWO-YEAR OLD

Thank you for your kind attention to Isabela yesterday. I appreciate your honoring her for who she is—a highly sensitive, intelligent child—and giving her the space to come to you and develop a relationship on her own terms. I recently attempted to find a pediatrician closer to my home that was referred to as "breastfeeding friendly." After trying to force her way through the examination of my now distraught daughter, she disdainfully observed me nurse Isabela to calm her. At one point, she said to Isabela while she was attempting to nurse, "Well, now, that's enough of that. We'll have none of that." At the end of the visit, this female pediatrician suggested I take Isabela out more in public to "overcome her phobias."

Isabela actually said in the parking lot when we left your office, "I like this doctor." She then waved goodbye from the car, saying "Bye-bye Doctor Punger." Last night she was checking my ears, and she allowed me to check hers.

–Lisa R.

COMFORTING HIM IN OUR "SPECIAL LITTLE WAY."

W e had our first experience with our son getting sick this week. He had a virus that caused him to run a fever and break out in a rash. He's over it now, and thanks to breastfeeding it never really got too bad. He nursed and nursed and nursed some more. It was wonderful to be able to soothe, comfort and care for him in our "special little way." Just when I think we've experienced breastfeeding to its fullest, something new happens, and I'm amazed by its endless provisions. I'll never be able to thank you enough for seeing us through the numerous challenges we faced initially. Breastfeeding my son has been all I'd hoped it would be... and more!

–Kimberly G.

A LETTER FROM PENNSYLVANIA

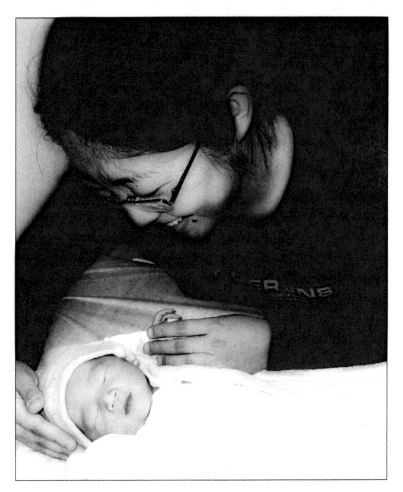

Hey, Johnny, WOW! I was just following a link from mothering.com and there you were!!! I read your whole website and was just blown away... I moved away just before you met Denise. My jaw just dropped when I saw your name and picture, and then even more so when I saw your practice's philosophy! We've been co-sleeping, extended-nursing and baby-wearing since our first son was born 8 1/2 years ago and would really have loved to have doctors like the two of you. I've been lucky in my midwives, but never have managed to find a sympathetic pediatrician or family practice doc. "I actually had one physician's assistant ask me how I could be nursing a two-year-old, saying "Doesn't the milk dry up after a year?""

I really enjoyed your wife's writings. I'd actually read the story of your footling breech during my last pregnancy without realizing it was your wife. Small world! I hope South Florida families appreciate how lucky they are. If you ever decide to move to Pennsylvania let me know and we'll be your first patients!

– Maureen M.

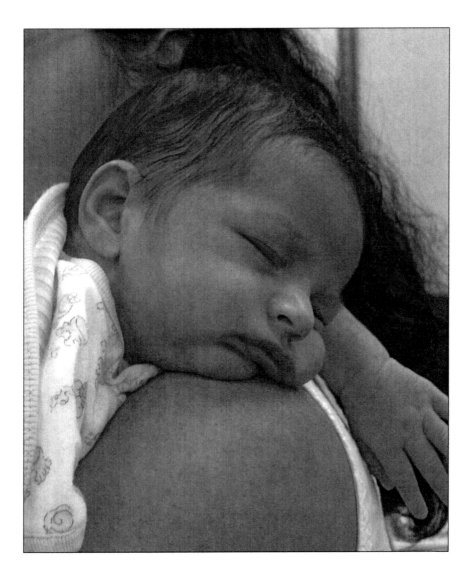

APPENDICES

APPENDIX A:

RESOURCES

I have included the sources that were useful to me at the appropriate times. Over the years the amount of resources continues to grow.

ORGANIZATIONS I BELONG TO

Coquelet & Punger Family Medicine, P.A. – http://twofloridadocs.com
American Academy of Family Practice – http://aafp.org
La Leche League International – http://lalecheleague.org
Academy of Breastfeeding Medicine – http://www.bfmed.org/

International Cesarean Awareness Network – http://www.ican-online.org
ILCA – http://www.ilca.org
Florida Lactation Consultant Association – http://www.flca.info
Florida Parenting Education Association – http://www.fpea.com

DOULA AND BIRTH ORGANIZATIONS

Mother to Mother – http://mothertomother.tripod.com
Gentle Spirit Doulas – http://gentlespiritdoulas.tripod.com
Midwifery Today Magazine – http://midwiferytoday.com
DONA International – http://www.dona.com
Childbirth and Postpartum Professional Association – http://www.cappa.net
Coalition to Improve Maternity Services – http://www.motherfriendly.org

BOOKS FOR BIRTH

Immaculate Deception by Suzanne Arms
Guide to Childbirth by Ina May Gaskin
Motherwit by Onnie Lee Logan
The Red Tent by Anita Diamant
Birthing from Within by Pam England
The Natural Pregnancy Book by Aviva Jill Romm
Baby Catcher: Chronicles of a Modern Midwife by Peggy Vincent

CHILDREN'S BOOKS

Runa's Birth by Uwe Spillmann and Inga Kamieth
Hello Baby! by Lizzy Rockewell
Mama Means Milk by Anne Marie Myers

NATURAL BREECH AND TWIN BIRTH

http://www.earthbirthproductions.com
http://www.midwiferytoday.com/articles/jerusalem.asp
http://www.birthchoice.info/index_files/breech.htm
http://www.birthingway.com/footling_breech.htm
Five years to the term breech trial: The rise and fall of a randomized

controlled trial (Glezerman, Obstetrics and Gynecology:Volume 194; Page 20; January 2006)

BREASTFEEDING BOOKS
Breastfeeding Your Priceless Gift to Your Baby and Yourself by Regina Sara Ryan, Deborah Auletta, Medical Advisor: Denise Punger
The Ultimate Breastfeeding Book of Answers by Jack Newman and Teresa Pitman
SEARS Parenting Library
Parenting from the Heart – published by motherwear.com
The Family Bed by Tine Thevenin

RESOURCES FOR SPECIAL BREASTFEEDING SITUATIONS

Tongue-Tie
Tongue-tie: Impact on Breastfeeding, Complete Management Including Frenotomy (video), by Evelyn Jain – http://drjain.com
Neonatal Ankyloglossia, The Academy of Breastfeeding Medicine Protocol – http://www.bfmed.org/ace-files/protocol/ankyloglossiaFinal_11.pdf
Frenulum Presentation by Brian Palmer – http://www.brianpalmerdds.com/frenum.htm
http://www.tonguetie.ballardscore.com
Congenital Tongue-Tie and Its Impact on Breastfeeding, by Elizabeth Coryllos, Catherine Watson Genna and Alexancer C. Salloum. American Academy of Pediatrics – http://www.aap.org/breastfeeding/8-27%20Newsletter.pdf

Duartes Galactosemia
http://www.genetics.emory.edu/ask/question.php?question_id=1057
http://www.lalecheleague.org/NB/NBJulAug97p123.html

MISCELLANEOUS TOPICS
Attachment Parenting International – http://www.attachmentparenting.com
Diaper Bags – http://www.banthebags.org

Babies at Work – http://www.babiesatwork.org

Milk Banks – http://www.hmbana.org/

Nutrition in Pregnancy – http://www.blueribbonbaby.org

Sedation Guidelines for Surgery –
   http://www.asahq.org/publicationsAndServices/NPO.pdf

Bed Sharing – http://www.bfmed.org/ace-files/protocol/cosleeping.pdf

Natural Family Planning – http://ccli.org

Dental –
   http://www.lalecheleague.org/llleaderweb/LV/LVAprMayJun06p27

Babywearing – http://www.wearyourbaby.com

Drugs and Breastfeeding (Dr. Tom Hale) – http://neonatal.ttuhsc.edu/lact

Pregnancy Memory Sculpture, LLC – http://www.geocities.com/pmsartist

Kangaroo Mother Care – http://kangaroomothercare.com/

Baby Friendly – http://www.babyfriendlyusa.org/

The Bradley Method – http://www.bradleybirth.com

Kellymom Breastfeeding and Parenting – http://www.kellymom.com

Breastfeeding after Reduction – http://bfar.org

Induced Lactation – http://www.asklenore.com

AAP Breastfeeding Statement –
   http://aappolicy.aappublications.org/cgi/content/full/pediatrics;115/2/496#SEC6

WHO Breastfeeding Statement –
   http://www.who.int/nutrition/topics/exclusive_breastfeeding/en/index.html

Newborn Jaundice – http://www.kellymom.com/newman/07jaundice.html

Lact-Aid Nursing Trainer System - http://www.lact-aid.com

International Board of Lactation Consultant Examiners –
   http://www.iblce.org

TORAH-BASED BIRTH RESOURCES

Teaching Your Children about God by Rabbi David Wolpe

http://www.rabbizions.com/

http://www.torahview.com/bris/html/the_bris.html

Doula Miriam Maslin – http://www.miriammaslin.com

JewishPregnancy.com – http://www.jewishpregnancy.org

Rabbinic Commentary – http://www.everburninglight.org/Shiprah-1.html

DVD

Birth Day – http://www.midwiferytoday.com/merchant2/merchant.mv

Born in Water– http://www.midwiferytoday.com/merchant2/merchant.mv

Dr. Jack Newman's Visual Guide to Breastfeeding –
  http://www.DrJackNewman.com

APPENDIX B:
HERBAL LABOR INDUCTIONS -
ARE THEY SAFE?

My third labor lasted easily over 12 hours giving me time to emotionally adjust to the escalating physical demands and surprise of my labor. Over and over, now that I am in private practice, I am hearing about intense labors that occur in two hours or less! Women often express delight about their miraculously quick labors (as if a quick labor were the goal). But I don't sense any emotional, physical, or spiritual satisfaction accompanying these seemingly precipitous deliveries.

The commonality I have noticed in these quick births is the use of herbals to bring on labor and augment contractions. I am all for the use of herbs in many conditions, but labor is not a condition and I can't support their use to hasten birth.

I've wondered why anyone who promotes homebirth would want to use herbs routinely to induce or augment labor. When I refer to "natural birth," I literally mean natural. A homebirth does not equal a "natural birth" if Blue and Black Cohosh are used to induce.

In my Breastfeeding Medicine based practice I see babies whose mothers report to me that they received various forms of cohosh in labor: teas, tinctures, and injections. I have noticed a trend with these homebirth babies. There is a tendency toward prematurity, cardiovascular distress, jaundice, meconium, failure to thrive, suck dysfunctions and hospitalizations. I also hear women bragging about the use of natural laxatives to bring on labor. Just like other prescription and non-prescription remedies, a laxative taken by the mother is a laxative an unborn child receives.

I understand that some midwives might say that use of these herbs is appropriate if a client is approaching 42 weeks, term rupture of membranes, or failure to progress. These herbs in most cases are probably safer than transport to a hospital. But I would stress that these are not routine situations, and the clients have a right to informed consent. Let's not be to cavalier about routine use.

APPENDIX C:
PREGNANCY AND LABOR - NO PICNIC FOR DAD
by John Coquelet DO

Now it is my turn to tell MY story. I will also share a few secrets that I know Denise hasn't told anyone. First of all, she tricked me into pregnancy. She wanted to work and travel, she said. I agreed, "Let's save our money and retire early." Next thing I know we are out of town, visiting relatives. It's December 25th. "Oh, John, I forgot to pack something and it's day fourteen." I knew better, but she was so "old" (30ish) and never pregnant, I thought all her eggs were dried up by now.

Two and a half weeks later, she tells me she is pregnant. "Yeah, right! Do another test and don't tell anyone until we are sure it's not a tumor." She did another test. It was still positive. But I really believed it when all the nausea and her complaining started at six weeks. I was going to be a father! So much for trips, cars and jet skis.

Most women will call a conveniently located obstetrician to establish care. Without considering other choices they will stick with the first OB they see. But not my wife. She wanted to tour a birthing center and meet their midwives.

"No way," I demanded. "You are a physician, and you are going to have an obstetrician deliver this baby." She has learned a lot about birth and midwifery since, so I'd never get away with spouting such uniformed opinions now.

In our training as physicians, we study the "condition" called pregnancy. Midwives, on the other hand, learn the bio-psycho-social model of birth. Denise had the worst pregnancy I ever thought possible. She cried all the time, and I do mean all the time. She needed someone who could deal with the psychosocial part a little better than her OB or I.

Her obstetrician would bring her into his office to counsel her, and Denise appreciated that. Her doctor jokingly admitted he wasn't a shrink, but he could show compassion. She complained to him that she could never raise a child.

"Why not?" he would ask.

"Because I hate cooking. How will I ever feed a kid?"

She stressed me out. I never wanted to live through another pregnancy with her. Everything I did was wrong. The phone bills were higher. Her sister Carrie in Seattle had just had a baby; so they were on the phone all the time commiserating.

To top off this difficult pregnancy, Denise had a partial placenta previa. This meant that the placenta was partly blocking the cervix; you know, the baby's way out. Denise's doctor took her out of work around her 33rd week. Then she just moped around the house, milking this pregnancy for all it was worth.

We were worried for a few weeks that Denise would need a c-section if the placenta did not migrate upward, and I knew she wanted a natural labor. The placenta did move, finally. What a relief! I easily see how so many couples get talked into induction (and are blind to all its risks) after a long burdensome, emotionally draining pregnancy.

This pregnancy ended with 22 hours of mortifying labor. Once again, we became concerned she would end up having a c-section, because she was exhausted and could not push. All I can tell you about father-coached labor is that it is not for me. I was caught in the middle of our two mothers. Mine passive and meek, and hers controlling. I felt like a servant who couldn't do anything right. Still, I was hoping our mothers could stay after the birth to help with baby William. I had to go back to work. Denise was recovering physically, and there was no one else to help her during the day.

Denise dwelled on this birth experience for a long time. If there is a Post

Traumatic Stress Disorder for labor, she had it. She had recurrent thoughts about what happened and what should have been.

It may seem hard to imagine now, but at the time she wasn't that interested in breastfeeding. Two things contributed to Denise's decision to breastfeed. One was that her sister Carrie was breastfeeding: she couldn't allow her younger sister have a life experience that she didn't share. The other was that I insisted she breastfeed. There was evidence to suggest nursing increases intelligence, and I wanted a smart boy! Also, of course, we could save money by not buying formula.

As she became proficient with it, though, Denise found reasons of her own for breastfeeding. It turned out to be healing for her. Although she still grieved for the birth experience she had wanted, breastfeeding reassured her that her body did not fail her or her baby. Besides, breastfeeding didn't involve any of that cooking she hated so much. I never thought we would have another wonderful son. Who could live through another pregnancy? We never discussed it much. Then one week she tells me, "If you want another baby, this is the weekend." That's all it took to get pregnant again.

During the next long 40 weeks Denise got into reading "birth books." She was determined to have a better experience. She told me she was going to find a doula. "A do-what?" She explained she was going to get someone that could help her have a better birth experience. That's when we met Bernadette. It took me two seconds to agree after we met her, "I want Denise to have a doula."

Let me tell you, I am frugal, but a doula was worth every penny. Denise's mind really was at ease about this, and so was mine. Dad, you may have the ability to be everything that your partner needs in labor (eight arms, physical strength of a mule, endurance and patience). If so, more power to you. I am glad we let the doula be all that. Not only did Bernadette help Denise, but she taught me how I could best meet Denise's needs.

The night that Denise went into labor with Scott I was already asleep, and she was quiet about it. She tells me she wanted me to be rested. I know she just didn't want me making her self-conscious. When I awoke a few hours later Denise, her sister Carrie and Bernadette were all in the kitchen. Denise says, "Get the shower stall ready; this baby is coming out now." Her doula says, "John, get the car ready. It's time to go to the hospital."

Knowing what Denise knows now, she would have had stayed home, but we all agreed it was better to stick with the planned agenda. I was getting nervous. She was having some serious pain, but Bernadette helped her. I wondered if Denise would deliver in my brand new SUV, but I got them both to the hospital in the knick of time.

I was surprised that on arrival to the hospital she gave birth immediately. The baby was a little blue. "See, Denise, I told you we needed the hospital." Later she explained he was probably blue because she resisted the urge to push during the drive.

Anyway, I was glad this delivery was over. Whatever the doula did to help Denise stay focused and relaxed worked. And I wasn't too tired to enjoy our new son or go get food. I have to be good at that, being married to someone who doesn't cook.

Denise has had the birth experience she hoped for: A labor in which she was in control and her feelings were validated. Now that she has hooked up with the doulas and is confident in birth, she wants another baby.

APPENDIX E:
WHY THE DASH?

As I was working on this book, a peer reviewer asked me about using a dash in naming the divine. She wondered if I was embarrassed about my beliefs. Here is an excerpt from my response, in case some of my readers are wondering the same thing:

Using the dash is a sign of respect in Judaism. How often do we hear, "Oh, GOD!" or "My GOD!" and similar exclamations? That is not a prayer, nor is it anything that speaker was conscious of saying. By using a dash, I feel that I am very conscious of my choice of words as I slow down and use a dash. And I feel more respectful. As you see, it "slowed" you down as the reader. You gave this subject some consideration and asked me for more information, rather than just quickly reading over it and not noticing what was being said. Anywhere I have left the spelling of G-d's name undashed, I was quoting someone else who had written it without a dash.

Apparently, my peer reviewer enjoyed my explanation. "I must say," she replied, "when I see your writings and see the 'dash,' you have to know it will make me smile, because you have taught me something. This I will treasure."

CPSIA information can be obtained at www.ICGtesting.com
Printed in the USA
LVOW110934230113

316908LV00004B/818/P